HOMEM🏠DE
LIVING

Home Dairy
with Ashley English

HOMEM🏠DE
LIVING

Home Dairy

with Ashley English

All You Need to Know to Make Cheese, Yogurt, Butter & More

LARK
CRAFTS

An Imprint of Sterling Publishing Co., Inc.
New York

WWW.LARKCRAFTS.COM

Senior Editor: Nicole McConville

Editorial Assistant: Beth Sweet

Creative Director: Chris Bryant

Layout & Design: Eric Stevens

Photographer: Lynne Harty

Cover Designer: Eric Stevens

Library of Congress Cataloging-in-Publication Data

English, Ashley, 1976-
  Homemade living : home dairy with Ashley English : all you need to know to make cheese, yogurt, butter & more / Ashley English.
      p. cm.
  Includes index.
  ISBN 978-1-60059-627-8 (hc-plc : alk. paper)
  I. Title.
  SF250.5.E56 2011
  637--dc22

                                                                2010020669

10 9 8 7 6 5 4 3 2 1

First Edition

Published by Lark Crafts
An imprint of Sterling Publishing Co., Inc.
387 Park Avenue South, New York, NY 10016

Text © 2011, Ashley English
Photography © 2011, Lark Crafts, An imprint of Sterling Publishing Co., Inc., unless otherwise specified
Illustrations © 2011, Lark Crafts, An imprint of Sterling Publishing Co., Inc., unless otherwise specified

Distributed in Canada by Sterling Publishing,
c/o Canadian Manda Group, 165 Dufferin Street
Toronto, Ontario, Canada M6K 3H6

Distributed in the United Kingdom by GMC Distribution Services,
Castle Place, 166 High Street, Lewes, East Sussex, England BN7 1XU

Distributed in Australia by Capricorn Link (Australia) Pty Ltd.,
P.O. Box 704, Windsor, NSW 2756 Australia

The written instructions, photographs, designs, patterns, and projects in this volume are intended for the personal use of the reader and may be reproduced for that purpose only. Any other use, especially commercial use, is forbidden under law without written permission of the copyright holder.

Every effort has been made to ensure that all the information in this book is accurate. However, due to differing conditions, tools, and individual skills, the publisher cannot be responsible for any injuries, losses, and other damages that may result from the use of the information in this book.

If you have questions or comments about this book, please contact:
Lark Crafts
67 Broadway
Asheville, NC 28801
828-253-0467

Manufactured in Canada

All rights reserved

ISBN 13: 978-1-60059-627-8

For information about custom editions, special sales, premium and corporate purchases, please contact Sterling Special Sales Department at 800-805-5489 or specialsales@sterlingpub.com.

For information about desk and examination copies available to college and university professors, requests must be submitted to academic@larkbooks.com. Our complete policy can be found at www.larkcrafts.com.

FSC
Mixed Sources
Product group from well-managed forests, controlled sources and recycled wood or fiber
Cert no. SW-COC-000952
www.fsc.org
© 1996 Forest Stewardship Council

✪ This book was printed on recycled paper with agri-based inks.

Table of Contents

Introduction

The interest in growing and making our own foods continues to gain momentum with every passing day. From rural homesteads to urban neighborhoods, people are picking up trowels, whisks, and pitchforks and learning to grow zucchini, keep a flock of laying chickens, and experiment with making their own yogurt. Perhaps you're one of the many who've begun canning batches of pickles and jams or taken on a hive of honeybees. Perhaps you'd like to become one of those people. No matter what path brought you to this point, you're now part of a community of individuals, all seeking to explore, tinker, delve, discuss, and revel in the excitement found in *Homemade Living*.

Making your own dairy products is one of the simplest and most cost-effective ways of getting a bit closer to the foods you eat. With a few gallons of milk and some friendly bacterial cultures, you can soon be indulging in your own artisan butter, yogurt, mozzarella, and more. No matter whether you keep milking animals yourself, know a dairy farmer down the way who's got milk to spare, or simply gather your milk fresh from the grocer, you'll soon learn that making dairy products is actually quite easy, rewarding, and unquestionably delicious.

My own interest in making dairy products at home came from a passage in Barbara Kingsolver's eminently inspiring *Animal, Vegetable, Miracle*. The part that catalyzed my dairy fervor was one in which she chronicled her family's experiment in mozzarella-making. I was hooked. "I can do that," I told myself. "I can make mozzarella magic happen in my kitchen." And so, I gathered up the necessary ingredients and equipment, took a deep breath, and got to work. When the formerly solid curd began to stretch and move with taffy-like elasticity, I was sold. I actually smiled at the pliant mass of milk before me, pleased, proud, and utterly smitten.

From there, it was really just a short leap to making a veritable feast of dairy products. I was having fun, tasting products of unparalleled (and inherently unique!) flavor and quality, and saving money all the while. And the best part?

I loved the "every-person" aspect of the craft—the fact that you can live anywhere and still produce delicious dairy products. No matter whether you're a city apartment dweller or an away-from-it-all denizen of the great outdoors, if you've got access to fresh milk, a source of heat, and a bit of cheesecloth, the pleasures of making your own dairy products are yours for the taking.

In this book, I share with you all the nitty-gritty details and learned-from-experience tips discovered along my own dairy-making journey. I've provided a primer on the history of home dairy-making, an overview of all the essential tools and equipment, a thorough examination of the ingredients involved, and a host of delectable recipes you can make for your family and friends. You'll also find plans for making your own cheese press; profiles of real people whipping up dairy bliss for fun, food, and finances; and some homespun body care recipes with dairy products featured front and center.

My sincerest desire is that this book provides you with just the right amount of instruction, creative challenge, and guidance to get you started on your own home dairy adventures. I took the plunge into this new way of living, and so can you, no matter if your kitchen is vast and expansive or more of a nook and cranny. Consider yourself forewarned, however, that dairy-making fever is deeply infectious and highly contagious. Once you get going, you (and quite possibly your friends and family!) might never be the same, and you'll possibly even wonder why it took you so long to get started in the first place.

Ashley English

ABOUT THE AUTHOR

A few years ago, I was hopping into my car each morning, heading off to a job in a medical office. Things changed, though, when a whirlwind romance quickly resulted in marriage, a little homestead at the end of a dirt road, and just the encouragement and support I needed to make some serious life changes. Combining my long-standing interest and education in nutrition, sustainability, and local food, I made the bold decision to leave my stable office job and try my hand at homesteading. It was a huge leap of faith, but I truly believed there was opportunity waiting in a simpler, pared-down life. My goal was to find ways to nourish both body and soul through mindful food practices. And so I jumped in, rubber boots first, completely unaware of what lay ahead.

To chronicle the triumphs and also the lessons— some humbling and some hilarious—of crafting a homemade life, I started up a blog, Small Measure (www.small-measure.blogspot.com). In it, I try to convey the same ideals I live every day: there are small, simple measures you can take to enhance your life while also caring for your family, community, and the larger world. It's been a trial-and-error experiment in living, encountering setbacks along with the joy. I've learned so much along the way, and I hope this book serves as continual encouragement for you, whether you want to try a little home dairying or are contemplating a more major leap of your own. If I did it, you certainly can, too.

Chapter 1
Creamery Origins

From the fields of Provence to the cliffs of Greece, from Turkish herders to Swiss milkmaids, dairy products are prized, lovingly crafted, and consumed with gusto the world over. In this chapter we'll explore the origins of our love affair with dairy and examine how dairy-making moved from the kitchen to the factory and back again.

IN THE BEGINNING

Humans have been dabbling with dairy products longer than we've been practicing agriculture. Our hunter-gatherer ancestors began animal domestication sometime around 11,000 B.C., starting with sheep and moving on to goats about 10,000 B.C. These animals, being small, nimble, and amenable to eating whatever scrubby, scraggly vegetation they encountered, could easily navigate cliffs, mountains, and other rugged terrain. Furthermore, they adapt readily to challenging weather, faring just as well in cold climates as more balmy ones.

While still nomadic, our tribal forebears would store surplus milk gathered from these sheep and goats in animal stomach pouches and head out on their daily hunts. Legend has it, one particularly auspicious day an Arabic nomad (or herder, or wandering merchant, depending on who's telling the tale) set out in the blazing heat of the desert sun, equipped with the day's milk ration. So the story goes, the heat of the sun interacted with the nomad's movements and the enzyme rennin (found inside the animal pouch), turning the milk to solid curds. Whether motivated by sheer curiosity or compelled by an empty stomach, the herder purportedly downed the foreign substance, immediately becoming the world's first *turophile*, or lover of cheese. I can't say I wouldn't have done the same.

The dawn of agriculture, when people literally started putting down roots (plant roots, that is), occurred around 9,000 B.C. in the Fertile Crescent, an area encompassing present-day Iraq, Syria, Lebanon, Israel, Kuwait, Jordan, southeastern Turkey, and parts of Iran. The permanence of these newly forming societies allowed for domestication of the larger, albeit fussier, cow. Though generous in terms of milk production, cows' needs are greater than those of the blithe sheep or the sprightly, make-do goat. Cows need shelter in poor weather and large tracts of verdant pasture for grazing. Its output being far superior to any of the other mammals humans attempted to milk, however, the sensitive cow became the go-to milker of choice.

SPREADING THE GOSPEL

Information on the nutritious, not to mention delicious, nature of milk began to spread. Manipulation of the milk provided by cows, sheep, goats, and other ruminants such as buffalo and yaks (that's right, yaks) began in earnest. While fresh milk is highly perishable, aging it not only preserves milk for later use, it arguably improves its flavor. What our ancestors couldn't use the same day, they could transform into a stable product to be stored for consumption or trade at another time. Use of dairy went global—a significant enough factor in ancient diets that it was etched onto walls, caves, and works of art. A Sumerian frieze from about 5000 B.C. depicts cows being milked, the milk in turn being strained, and then the resulting substance being churned into butter. Later clay tablets show milk being rendered into cheese. Ancient Egypt was in on the dairy action, as well. Unearthed artifacts depict cheese and dairy products as staples of daily life.

Greek mythology also includes reference to cheese, most notably in Homer's *Odyssey*. When investigating Cyclops's cave, Odysseus and his men discover pens holding an abundance of goats and sheep, wicker baskets for molding cheese, and racks of curing cheese. The typical cheeses being produced in that hot, humid region at that time were highly salted in order to preserve them. These early cheeses would have been similar to feta and cottage, or other soft, salty cheeses, served fresh and intended to be eaten soon after they were made.

Dairying made its way to Rome, where inventive Romans expanded and improved on cheese-making techniques. They designed a type of cheese press, developed the process of ripening, and experimented with flavor enhancements such as smoking. Home cheese-making was widely practiced by Roman citizens, so much so that a number of larger homes contained kitchens expressly reserved for the production of cheese and other areas devoted to cheese ripening. Additionally, the Romans developed the practice of adding rennet to milk to hasten coagulation. This discovery, along with the cheese press, allowed curds to be pressed into hard cheeses. At the height of the Roman Empire, Italy was unquestionably the epicenter of cheese-making, for both home and market. Perhaps the secret to the Romans' seemingly infinite inventiveness was abundant cheese and dairy consumption!

BLESSED ARE THE CHEESE-MAKERS

Roman colonization took cheese out of Italy and across all of Europe. As the legions conquered outlying territories, they adapted, invented, and spread agricultural and culinary practices. When the Roman Empire began to decline, much of the trade of commodities over long distances fell apart as well. Cheese-making was a casualty of Rome's demise, with few advances in technique or production occurring during the Middle Ages. Fortunately, however, Catholic monasteries served as repositories of information for all things food related, from growing to harvesting to preserving. Monks revived cheese and dairy-making practices, and crafted beers and wines with ingredients indigenous to their locale (and you thought monasteries were all vespers and lauds). They also experimented with new methods of curing, leading to advancements in ripening techniques and mold-rind cheeses such as Brie and Camembert.

GOD SAVE THE CHEESE

Monasteries and abbeys left a profound and enduring legacy of cheese-making in the British Isles. England, Scotland, Wales, Ireland, and the outlying smaller islands possess ideal conditions for dairying. The temperature, terrain, elevation, and highly fertile grasslands are eminently conducive to the needs of grazing animals (not to mention languid picnicking and Jane Austen novels). Some of the most famous English cheeses include Wensleydale (Yorkshire), Cheshire (Cheshire County), Stilton (Leicestershire), and cheddar (Somerset).

COTTAGE (CHEESE) INDUSTRY

By the later Middle Ages, the production and manufacture of cheese and other dairy products began making their way out of monasteries and home kitchens exclusively and into modest cottage industries. It was during this time, and in the ensuing years, that cheddar, Parmesan, Gouda, and Camembert showed up on the global cheese board. In mountain communities of the Jura and Alps, dairy associations and cooperatives were formed to exchange information about the best ways to craft a quality cheese.

Later, whole villages and even regions caught cheese-making fever, realizing the potential benefit of having a regionally recognized commodity of fine repute. Cooperatives formed during the 13th through 16th centuries introduced cheeses such as Gruyère and Emmentaler, both from Switzerland. The reputation and legacy of these items provided Swiss cheese-makers with the confidence to begin making their dairy products en masse in the early 19th century, opening the world's first cheese factory in Bern in 1815.

BRAVE NEW WORLD

In the early 17th century, several waves of English immigrants arrived in North America, bringing their dairying and cheese-making practices with them. They also brought cows, first to Jamestown Colony in 1611 and then to Plymouth Colony in 1624. British influence on the practice of American cheese-making has been particularly strong. Many cheeses made in New England are reflective of British styles, most notably cheddar.

In other areas of North America where Swiss, German, and Scandinavian immigrants settled, such as the Midwest states, dairy products produced there similarly reflect a European heritage. Emmentalers and other Swiss styles were among the first cheeses to be regularly manufactured and consumed in that region. Italian, German, French, English, and Dutch immigrants brought their offerings to the upper Midwest states, as well, including mozzarella, Muenster, Brie, cheddar, and Gouda. Enterprising Wisconsin-based cheese-makers also experimented with new cheese-making styles, creating brick and Colby cheeses. In Quebec, where a number of French immigrants settled, Francophile cheeses are the order of the day. Other areas of Canada reflect a British influence, crafting a number of cheddars.

International Flavor

Dairy products can be found all over the world. Just about every culture and continent uses dairy items in one form or another. From sheep, goats, and cows to water buffalo, horses, and yaks, animal milk is transformed into myriad foodstuffs for humans to enjoy.

This fairly comprehensive—though far from exhaustive—chart lists dairy products by the manner in which they are processed. While many might be familiar to you, others may perhaps be a bit more exotic. Kumis, anyone? (That's fermented horse milk, for the uninitiated.)

BUTTER PRODUCTS

butterfat
clarified butter/ghee
cultured butter
mild cultured butter
raw cream butter
sweet cream butter
whey butter

CHEESE TYPES

blue vein/moldy
brined
cream
fresh
hard
khoa
mascarpone
pasta filata/pulled-curd
semi-hard
semi-soft
soft/soft-ripened
sour milk
whey

CREAM PRODUCTS

clotted cream
condensed cream
crème fraîche
double cream
half-and-half
kaymak
pasteurized cream
smetana
sour cream
table cream
whipping cream

FROZEN PRODUCTS

frozen custard
frozen yogurt
gelato
ice cream
ice milk

MILK TYPES

baked milk
condensed/evaporated milk
condensed/evaporated part-skimmed milk
condensed/evaporated skimmed milk
extended shelf life milk (ESL)
low-fat milk
low-fat/skim raw milk
pasteurized milk
raw milk
skim milk
sterilized milk
ultra high temperature milk (UHT)
whole milk

POWDERED MILK PRODUCTS

infant formula
powdered goat milk
powdered milk
powdered skim milk
powdered whey

SOUR MILK PRODUCTS

ayran
buttermilk
cheese curd
cream yogurt
filmjölk
kefir
kumis/airag
lassi
piimä
quark
soured milk
viili
yogurt
yogurt, mild

WHEY PRODUCTS

sour whey
sweet whey

A DAIRY-MAKING REVOLUTION

During the late 18th and 19th centuries, advances in industrial technology introduced a huge shift that occurred in the way goods were created and labor was performed. Coal-fired steam power was followed by the invention of the internal combustion engine and, later, electric power. Work previously performed manually was given to machines. Waterways were more easily dug and roads chiseled through heretofore impenetrable mountains, allowing agriculture to flourish and perishable commodities to be shipped from one location to another.

The new technologies moved dairy-making out of small farms, creameries, and home kitchens and into factories, where vast machines could crank out thousands of pounds of butter and cheese daily. Refrigeration allowed milk to be preserved until ready for use, allowing processing to occur far from remote dairy farms. Cold shipping and rapid transit allowed dairy products to be sold and consumed far from both pasture and factory.

COMMON GROUND

There was a time when keeping a family cow was an everyday practice, witnessed as commonly as the sight of chickens scratching in the yard and laundry drying in the breeze. In Britain, and to a lesser extent in early colonial America in areas such as Boston, those that couldn't afford to own property were allowed to make use of common land, sometimes referred to as the "commons." Many peasants used the commons to graze livestock, ensuring access to a reliable source of milk and meat for their families.

Over time, however, many commons were appropriated from public use and developed into areas of private ownership. As public access to grazing lands decreased, those who couldn't purchase property lost the ability to keep milking animals. Purchasing milk could be prohibitively expensive, and the ability to craft homemade dairy products was out of the reach of many. In the United States, the family cow in the backyard was supplanted by

the subdivision and suburban landscape. Land just off the fringes of urban areas was parceled up and converted to housing. Backyards were modest and could hardly accommodate the needs of a cow.

In more recent years, a renewed interest in locally sourced, artisan, and homemade foods has sparked a return to home-based dairy production. Regardless of the presence of a milking animal in the backyard, home cooks are once again practicing the craft of DIY dairy, culturing yogurt and ripening feta cheese in their kitchens. Furthermore, small creameries continue to crop up in every region, with a host of enthusiastic fans ready to gobble up their products and learn about the practice of small-scale dairy-making.

Chapter 2
Ingredients:
Milking the Subject

When selecting ingredients for home dairy-making, seek out the best quality items you can find. Your finished product can only be as good as its component parts, so be certain to start with premium offerings. Milk is a highly perishable food (before it's preserved, that is). Select the freshest, cleanest milk you can find from a supplier you trust, and get ready to be amazed by the flavor, texture, and diversity of dairy deliciousness coming out of your kitchen. Patting yourself on the back upon completion of said dairy products is entirely optional.

MILK

The basis of all dairy products, milk is the most essential ingredient in the home dairy kitchen. Just as grain is necessary to produce bread and fruit to create wine, milk is indispensable for making cheese, yogurt, kefir, ice cream, and more. All this delicious diversity arises from one basic ingredient: animal milk. (While nondairy options made of everything from soy to nuts to hemp may be found at your local market, they are made through different processes that are beyond the scope of this book.)

Dairy products the world over are made from a variety of milks. If an animal produces milk, humans have tried their hand at extracting it: cows, goats, sheep, water buffalo, caribou, camels, donkeys, moose, reindeer, horses, buffalo, and even llamas. The composition of milk, while varying from animal to animal, is largely made up of the same basic elements in differing quantities: water (comprising the bulk of milk's composition), proteins, fat (butterfat), lactose (milk sugar), vitamins, and minerals. The recipes herein were developed and tested using cow and goat milk.

For many of you, the milk you'll be using to make home dairy items will be picked up at your nearest grocer. In that case, it's likely to have been both pasteurized and homogenized. **Pasteurization**, named after French chemist and biologist Louis Pasteur, is a process that greatly slows the growth of microbes in food. Introduced in the 19th century, pasteurization doesn't completely kill microorganisms in the same way that sterilization does. Instead, it curtails the number of pathogens (microorganisms likely to cause disease), so long as a food, once pasteurized, is refrigerated and consumed in an expedient manner. Beyond killing the bacteria that can make you sick, pasteurization also kills beneficial bacteria in milk that are necessary to certain chemical reactions in the process of making cheese or cultured dairy products. Therefore, if you intend to make these products using pasteurized milk, it will be necessary to add starter culture to replace the missing bacteria.

Homogenization is the process used to combine two insoluble substances into an emulsion. You know how oil and vinegar have a natural tendency to separate from each other in your bottle of homemade vinaigrette? That's on account of their lack of homogenization. Had they been homogenized, the oil would have been broken up into particles small enough to penetrate the vinegar. The same thing happens with milk. Homogenization punctures the butterfat particles in milk, which are then made small enough to no longer separate from the water, creating a uniform distribution of butterfat within the liquid.

It is homogenization that creates the percentage designations indicated on grocery store milk. **Skim milk** (also referred to as "fat-free" in some countries, as the remaining percentage of fat is considered negligible) literally has the cream skimmed off the top and, once homogenized, contains a butterfat content of no more than 0.5 percent. Skim milk is used in making starter culture, as well as in hard cheeses like Romano and Parmesan. **Low-fat milk**, after homogenization, has between 1 and 2 percent butterfat remaining, while **whole milk** retains all of its original butterfat, with a percentage between 3.5 and 4 percent.

The Raw and the Cooked: Raw versus Pasteurized Milk

If you have access to fresh, raw, unadulterated, unprocessed milk, consider yourself blessed by the dairy gods. Raw milk possesses a number of attributes that are otherwise destroyed or reduced during pasteurization, including beneficial bacteria (such as lactic acids), heat-sensitive enzymes (including lactase, lipase, and phosphatase), and vitamins A, B_6, and C (all heat-sensitive nutrients). That said, if you have any reservations whatsoever about the purity of your milk or sanitary practices at its dairy of origin, you will want to pasteurize it. Potentially harmful bacteria can be found in raw milk, including mycobacterium (responsible for tuberculosis—characterized by difficulty breathing, wheezing, and chest pain), brucella (responsible for brucellosis—characterized by fever and joint pain), and salmonella (responsible for salmonellosis—characterized by abdominal pain, vomiting, and diarrhea). Some of these bacteria have also shown up in pasteurized milk.

Essentially, the hygiene standards practiced on the farm will determine what sort of opportunistic bacteria can contaminate the milk. These bacteria pose the greatest health threat to children, seniors, and those with vulnerable immune systems. That said, if you are utterly certain about the cleanliness of your milk—either because you are well-acquainted with your dairy supplier or you keep dairy animals yourself and are a hygiene ninja—you may choose to forego pasteurization. Many raw milk advocates say pasteurization compromises flavor and texture, as the process destroys enzymes and makes proteins, vitamins, and minerals less available chemically.

Rules and regulations concerning the sale and consumption of raw milk and raw milk products vary widely. To learn about raw milk in your area, visit www.realmilk.com (U.S. and international information is provided). Consider the pros and cons of raw versus pasteurized milk to make the most informed decision for yourself and your family.

Home Pasteurization

Pasteurizing raw milk at home is easy, as long as you make certain to practice scrupulous hygiene. Prepare all of your equipment in advance by washing it in hot, soapy water and then allowing to air dry, make sure your kitchen is as clean as it can possibly be (no need to bust out the bleach, simply make sure countertops are clean; I use a homemade vinegar and water solution), and keep your raw milk refrigerated until you're ready to begin.

TO PREPARE:

1. Sterilize a stainless-steel stockpot by rinsing your pot with the hottest tap water. Add several inches of water to another, larger, stockpot. Add the milk you'll be using to the smaller pot. Place the smaller pot inside the larger one, making sure the water doesn't touch the bottom of the interior pot.

2. Gradually heat the milk to 145°F (63°C), checking the temperature with a dairy thermometer. Once the milk has come to temperature, set a timer for 30 minutes. Keep the milk at a consistent temperature the entire time, stirring the pot every so often to ensure even distribution of heat. If an interruption takes you out of the kitchen and you return to find the temperature has fallen, you'll have to start the timing from the beginning.

3. While your milk heats, clean your sink to a sparkle and fill it with ice and cold water, about as deep as your milk pot, to make a water bath. When the timer goes off, submerge the pot containing the milk into the bath.

4. Stir the milk continually until the temperature drops to 40 to 45°F (4 to 7°C). You want this to happen fairly rapidly, so be sure the water bath is really cold and full of ice when you submerge the milk-filled pot.

5. Once the milk has cooled, transfer it to a clean, covered container. Store in the refrigerator for up to two weeks.

STARTER CULTURES

The name gives away the role of this essential dairy-making ingredient. Used to make everything from cheese to yogurt, kefir, and sour cream, starter cultures are what get things started, as it were, in your pot of milk. Bacteria in the culture gobbles up lactose (milk sugars) and gives off lactic acid, jump-starting the acidification process. Lactic acid is essential for curdling milk, the first step in many home dairy recipes. Starter cultures also greatly influence the taste, smell, and physical structure of finished dairy products.

While there is a great deal of variety in the actual cultures used in home dairy-making, there are two basic types: mesophilic and thermophilic. Within those two categories, starter cultures may be referred to as traditional (mother culture) or direct-set (DVI). Let's examine the two main categories and both forms they come in.

Mesophilic Cultures

Mesophilic starter cultures don't do well if heated beyond 103°F (39°C). Just remember, mesophilic "loves cool." Mesophilic cultures are therefore used to make buttermilk and cheeses preferring low milk and curd temperatures, such as Gouda, cheddar, and feta. When this form of starter culture is required, the recipe you are using will indicate it.

It's acceptable to use any mesophilic culture; however, there are some specified varieties available within the broader category. So, for example, you might use one culture to make Brie, Camembert, Havarti, Gouda, Edam, feta, blue cheese, or chèvre, whereas a completely different culture might be more suitable for making cheddar, Colby, or Monterey Jack. It's not as confusing as it seems. Most suppliers specializing in cheese-making equipment will provide information for choosing the best mesophilic culture to create whatever product you have in mind (see page 129 for a list of suppliers).

Thermophilic Cultures

These starter cultures can take the heat. Thermophilic cultures are fine at temperatures up to 132°F (56°C). Just remember, thermophilic "loves warmth." Thermophilic cultures are key to the production of yogurt and hard Italian cheeses such as Parmesan and Romano, as well as Swiss-type cheeses. Whatever recipe you are following will indicate if you should be using a thermophilic culture. Also, thermophilic cultures have variations especially suited for achieving the best possible form of whatever dairy product you might be creating. Chat with your local cheese-making vendor or read over the options listed on dairy-making websites to find the option that best suits your needs.

Traditional (Mother) Cultures

Throughout history, part of the cheese-maker's art has been in the care and feeding of a "mother" bacterial culture. Once the "mother" is ready, she can produce "offspring" for as long as she is "fertile," to really stretch the metaphor. Traditional cultures can be a bit more demanding than direct-set cultures, as they require a lengthy culturing time before they can be used, usually somewhere between 15 and 24 hours for mesophilic cultures and 6 to 8 hours for thermophilic cultures. Once made, frozen mother culture will keep its vitality for up to one month. After that, you'll have to make up a fresh batch.

Starter cultures

DIY Mother Culture

If you'd like to make your own batch of traditional culture, follow these simple instructions. Either thermophilic or mesophilic mother cultures can be made using this method, although each type requires a different incubation temperature.

TO PREPARE:

1. First, sterilize your vessel: Fill a large stockpot with enough water to cover a 1 quart Mason jar. Submerge a clean jar in the pot, allowing water to fill it, and cover the jar with a lid and screw band. Bring the water to a boil over high heat, and boil rapidly for 5 minutes. Remove the jar from the pot, uncap, and empty the water inside back into the pot.

2. Allow the jar to cool slightly. Fill the jar with skim milk, leaving ½ inch headspace between the top of the milk and the underside of the secured lid.
NOTE: Be sure to give the jar a little bit of cooling-off time before filling with milk, otherwise the temperature variation between the hot jar and the cold milk may cause the jar to crack.

3. Place the milk-filled jar back into the stockpot. Bring the water to a boil over high heat, reduce heat to medium-high, and boil for 30 minutes. This will sterilize the milk, killing off unwanted bacteria while allowing the mother culture to thrive.

4. Remove the jar from the stockpot and place on a kitchen cloth in a protected area away from drafts. Let the milk cool to 108 to 110° F (42 to 43°C) for thermophilic culture or 70 to 72°F (21 to 22°C) for mesophilic culture.

5. Add the contents of one freeze-dried packet of mesophilic or thermophilic culture (depending on what type of mother culture you intend to produce) to the jar of cooled milk. Place the lid and screw band back on, and shake the jar lightly for a couple of minutes, just enough to distribute the culture throughout the milk.

6. Keep the jar in an area where its internal temperature can remain somewhat constant, such as a kitchen pantry or cabinet. If it seems too cool, consider wrapping the jar with a towel. Allow the milk to inoculate at 108 to 110°F (42 to 43°C) for 6 hours if making thermophilic culture or 70 to 72°F (21 to 22°C) for 18 hours if making mesophilic culture. See Incubating Ideas on page 55 for ideas on regulating temperatures. Check the culture after those respective inoculation periods. If it doesn't seem to be coagulating, leave it for another 6 hours or so, making sure to regulate the temperature. This part of the process is known as "ripening."

7. Once the mother starts to look like yogurt, sort of gelatinous and firm, and pulls away easily from the jar's edge, put it straight into the refrigerator. If you don't get to making cheese right away, that's fine; you can keep your mother in the fridge for up to 3 days. After that, it needs to be frozen.

8. To freeze your mother culture, run 5 or 6 empty ice cube trays under extremely hot tap water (wear rubber gloves!) for about 1 minute. Spoon the refrigerated mother into the trays, and cover the trays with plastic wrap. Place the trays in the freezer and allow to freeze solid, which should take 3 to 4 hours. Don't forget about them, because once they're firm, you'll need to transfer them to a resealable freezer bag.

9. Mark the bag with the date. Frozen mother culture will be good for about a month.

Direct-set Cultures (DVIs)

Developed in the 1980s, this time-saving technology is to home dairy makers what commercially produced pectin is to home canners. Direct-set cultures, also known as direct-vat inoculants (DVIs), are made in a laboratory and contain all of the important characteristics found in traditionally made cultures without the need to first be cultured. Available in powdered form and stored in the freezer until you need them, direct-set cultures are simply added to warmed milk. Many come in single-use packages, intended to work in 2 gallons of milk. It is also possible to purchase direct-set cultures in bulk, measuring out the amount of powder required for larger or smaller batches. If measuring from bulk powder, use this guide to determine how much you'll need:

Bulk Direct-set Culture

$1/8$ teaspoon per 1 gallon milk
$1/4$ teaspoon per 2 to 5 gallons milk
$1/2$ teaspoon per 5 to 10 gallons milk

RENNET

A collection of naturally occurring enzymes, rennet is found in the stomach of any mammal, helping it to digest mother's milk. One protein-digesting enzyme in particular, chymosin (or rennin), coagulates milk, separating curds, or solids, from whey, the liquid portion of milk. Essential for mammalian digestion, the role of rennet is equally important in cheese-making. While milk would naturally separate into curds and whey if left alone for several days, it would also become a bit tangy and acidic, not the ideal flavor to begin with when making cheese (although such a flavor is desirable later, during ripening and maturing). Adding rennet to milk while it is still sweet and fresh expedites coagulation while keeping the fresh flavor intact.

As discussed in the opening chapter, the action of rennet is rumored to have been discovered by a wandering nomad, who found solids in his milk pouch when he'd started his day with liquid. This discovery

Organic

Organic foods are produced without the use of chemicals. Crops must be grown without the use of pesticides, herbicides, and nonorganic fertilizers. All organic products, including those derived from animals, must be free of antibiotics, artificial growth hormones, genetically modified organisms (GMOs), irradiation, and sewage waste. Furthermore, the production of organic foods cannot involve the use of cloned animals, artificial ingredients, or synthetic preservatives.

Organic milk is certified to be free of rBGH (or rBST), a bovine growth hormone used to boost milk production in cows; additionally, milk may only be organically certified if the cows were given no antibiotics, their feed was free of pesticides, and they were permitted access to pasture. Cows that have been treated with rBGH produce such an exaggerated amount of milk that they must be milked three times a day. As a result, many cows experience mastitis, an infection of the udder, and a reduced lifespan. Furthermore, the milk from rBGH-treated cows has been shown to contain IGF-1, a growth hormone shared by humans. Human ingestion of dietary IGF-1 via hormone-addled milk may cause a proliferation of cancer-causing cells, especially affecting reproductive organs sensitive to hormonal fluctuations.

In the United States, federally mandated standards require that third-party state or private agencies oversee organic certification for producers. The U.S. Department of Agriculture (USDA) in turn accredits these agencies. In order for a farm or dairy to become certified organic, the land and animals must not have encountered any prohibited materials for three years. Scrupulous recordkeeping must be on hand to prove this, in addition to a detailed plan for preventing contamination by nonorganic materials. A number of agencies around the world perform similar organic certification testing. Requirements, regulations, and oversight vary from country to country but are, for the most part, quite similar.

led to widespread use of animal stomachs for cheese coagulation. Along the way, it was discovered that the fourth chamber (abomasums) of a young kid or calf was particularly adept at producing rennet. After animals were slaughtered, the abomasums were cut up into strips, salted, dried, and added in small portions to milk to speed up the separation of curds and whey. This bit of dried stomach was later dubbed *rennen* by the Germans, defined as "running together," eventually becoming known in modern parlance as rennet. Rennet is now sold in powdered, tablet, and liquid form. Rennet is standardized, so all forms work equally well. Personally, I prefer liquid, as it's quite easy to measure. Rennet is perishable; store tablets and powder in the freezer and liquid forms in the refrigerator.

Animal Rennet

Though largely abandoned in favor of standardized, synthesized rennet, some cheese-makers in parts of Europe still use rennet in

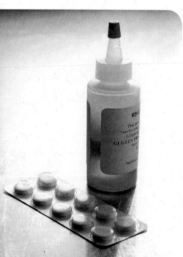

the traditional manner. The stomachs of young calves are cut and then added to either saltwater or whey, along with vinegar or wine. The addition of acid allows rennet production to flourish. The solution is left for several days and then filtered. The pieces of stomach are dried and then broken into small pieces to be reconstituted as needed for cheese-making.

Vegetable Rennet

Throughout history, when animal sources of rennet have been scarce, plant-based sources of coagulating enzymes have been sought out as alternatives. The ancients used everything from fig juice to nettles, thistles, and mallow.

Today, commercially available vegetable rennet is made with an enzyme produced by the mold *Mucor miehei*. This mold contains chymosin (the active constituent responsible for causing the separation of curds from whey), and is identical to animal rennet in chemical structure.

Genetically Manufactured Rennet

Right up until the early 1990s, rennet was made in the tried and true fashion, with either abomasums or vegetables known for their coagulating properties. Nowadays, however, most rennet is genetically manufactured via bacteria into which the enzyme for rennet has been introduced. Grown in huge vats, these bacteria produce rennet as a byproduct, which is then extracted, purified, and sold for cheese-making.

LIPASE

Lipase is an enzyme made by certain animals (including humans), to break down dietary fats during digestion. In the home dairy, the role of lipase is to impart certain types of cheeses with their characteristic strong flavors. Raw milk naturally contains lipase enzymes, which act on triglycerides found in milk fat, freeing up fatty acids. Add in ripening time and you've got nuanced flavors that distinguish certain cheeses.

Pasteurization deactivates lipase, however. If you're using pasteurized milk in home cheese-making, then the addition of commercially prepared lipase is essential. Without it, the flavors associated with many types of cheeses will be almost completely absent. Vegetarians should know that most commercially produced lipases used in cheese-making are animal derived, although microbially sourced varieties do exist.

Two of the most commonly available varieties of lipase are Italase (mild), which is customarily added to blue, mozzarella, Parmesan, and certain other cheeses, and Capilase (sharp), which is used for Romano, provolone, and other strongly flavored cheeses.

BACTERIA & MOLDS

Some cheeses require the artificial introduction of specialized molds to give them their characteristic flavor and appearance. These molds are really fungi or bacteria that are crucial in making, say, the Roquefort cheese taste and look as we've come to expect. Added molds will appear either internally, such as the mold that makes "eyes" develop in Swiss cheeses, or externally, evidenced by the bloomy rind on Brie. Molds used in cheese-making can be purchased through a cheese-making supplier.

Penicillium candidum

When you think of the rind on a wheel of Brie, you're thinking of this mold. *Penicillium candidum* is used to ripen Brie, Coulommiers, Sainte-Maure, and some French-style goat cheeses. After the mold is sprayed onto the surface of the curd, it spreads and grows incredibly quickly, keeping other molds from developing in the process. It is then allowed to age, during which time its characteristic white bloomy rind forms. The rind actually begins as tiny, fine,

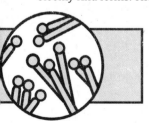

white hairs that grow and overlap and come to resemble what the French call *poil de chat*, or cat fur. Tasty, no? This fur is then rubbed away, leaving only a thin white rind behind that acts as a protective enclosure for the cheese's soft interior. *Penicillium candidum* also contributes to the development of flavor during the ripening stage. This surface mold, given the proper salt and moisture, will develop a rind that breaks down amino acid chains from the outside in, creating an increasingly soft, buttery texture with time.

Thin white rind of *Penicillium camemberti*

Penicillium camemberti

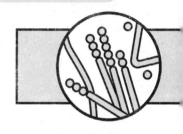

This mold is quite similar to *Penicillium candidum*, producing many parallels in characteristic flavor and appearance. *Penicillium camemberti*, however, is used more often in producing goat's milk (as opposed to cow's milk) soft cheeses.

Penicillium roqueforti

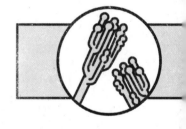

When the first blue cheeses were made, *Penicillium roqueforti* was literally in the air. Early European cheese-makers found the mold on and in their cheeses when they were left in caves, such as those in Roquefort, France, to age. Now available in both fast and very-fast growing forms, *Penicillium roqueforti* is used in the manufacture of Stilton, Roquefort, Gorgonzola, Danablu, and other blue cheeses.

The telltale blue veins of *Penicillium roqueforti*

The mold imparts the characteristic blue-green ripple typical of such cheeses, along with a smooth, creamy, spreadable texture. Enzymes created by *Penicillium roqueforti* are responsible for the pleasingly pungent flavor and aroma associated with blue cheeses. These enzymes break down complex molecules into simple ones, changing the fibrous chemical structure into a smoother one and imbuing it with piquant flavor and smell.

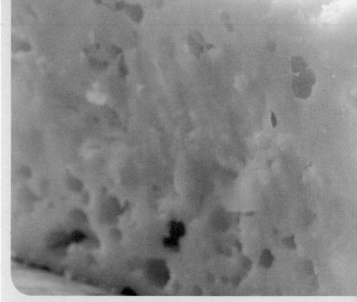

Brevibacterium linens

B. *linens* is a red mold, used to create orange and yellow coloration on cheese surfaces. Often referred to as "red cultures," it develops quickly and assists with ripening. The mold is added to the brining mix and sprayed onto washed-rind cheeses

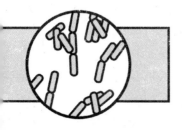

during aging. The sulfurous aromas produced by the mold are characteristic of brick, Limburger, and Muenster cheeses. Which is to say, when you smell "stinky cheese," *Brevibacterium linens* are shouting "Hello! We're here!"

Brevibacterium linens at work

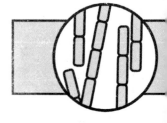

The "eyes" formed by *Propionic shermanii*

Propionic shermanii

Propionic shermanii is responsible for putting the holes (or "eyes"), smell, and taste into Swiss, Emmentaler, and Gruyère cheeses. Without it, many "hole-y" cheeses would be downright secular!

Geotrichum candidum

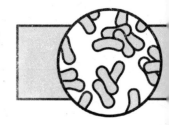

This mold plays a key role in cheese ripening. Used in conjunction with other molds, *Geotrichum candidum* contributes to both flavor and physical integrity during the ripening process of cheeses such as Brie and Camembert. It is also used in ripening for some goat cheeses. The mold helps to create a neutral environment in which *Penicillium candidum* and *Brevibacterium linens* can flourish and do their thing.

FLAKE SALT

Salt is an essential ingredient in the home dairy, especially when making cheese. Through its hygroscopic properties, salt is able to pull liquid out of cheese curds and into the

Flake salt

Bottled lemon juice and citric acid

whey, which is then drained off. Flake salt is usually added right before pressing to help pull out any remaining moisture left inside the curds. Salt also reduces the size of curds, making them easier to press and retain their form.

When it pulls moisture out of foods, salt also pulls moisture away from bacteria, making it difficult for them to survive. Added near the end of the cheese-making process, flake salt prevents any opportunistic bacteria that may have sneakily made their way into the milk from thriving. It also slows down the growth rate of lactic bacteria. And, of course, salt adds flavor. Some cheeses, such as feta, simply wouldn't be themselves without the addition of salt.

In home dairy-making, you'll need to use flake salt, the granules of which are slightly larger than table salt or sea salt. Flake salt (also known as cheese-making salt) is a coarse, non-iodized salt that dissolves completely in water, leaving behind no grit, grains, or residue of any kind. Selecting salt without added iodine is particularly important, as its presence can kill off some cultures and slows down the cheese aging process. Flake salt can be obtained from cheese-making suppliers; you can also use ground Kosher or canning salt with equal success. Whichever salt you use, be sure that it contains no anticaking ingredients.

ACIDS

A number of supplemental acids may be called for in home dairy-making, including vinegar, citric acid, tartaric acid, and lemon juice. Citric and tartaric acids can be found at dairy-making suppliers, as well as at some natural foods stores. When using lemon juice, I suggest bottled organic juice, as its acidity level will be more consistent than fresh-squeezed juice.

HERBS, SPICES & FLAVORINGS

A number of homemade dairy products benefit from the addition of herbs and spices. I'm thinking of a particular Gouda I'm crazy about that is studded throughout with cumin seeds. Then there's that cheddar with the sage…I could go on and on. The point here is that, since you're in

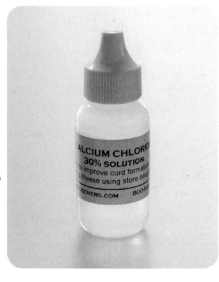

present in milk, which, in turn, can hinder the ability of rennet to coagulate properly. You might end up with an oozy, gooey, milky mess that fails to firm up and cooperate like a good cheese should. The shortcut around this difficulty is to add calcium back in the form of calcium chloride. For each gallon of milk called for in your recipe, add $1/4$ teaspoon of calcium chloride, diluted in $1/4$ cup of cool water. Stir the mixture into warmed milk before you add in your starter culture. Calcium chloride is available in both powdered and liquid forms from cheese-making suppliers.

charge of your home dairy, you can be as extravagant or as judicious as you'd like with flavor flourishes. For added heat, toss in dried chili flakes. Try cumin, caraway, mustard seeds, or juniper berries in hard cheeses, or basil, marjoram, oregano, chives, thyme, dill, garlic, sage, tarragon, or chervil in soft cheeses. Explore and discover which flavors speak to you. Herbs are best used fresh, but if fresh herbs are hard to come by, dried can work reasonably well. For each tablespoon of fresh herb called for, use one teaspoon dried.

Consider add-ins to yogurt or ice cream. Fresh fruit or a spoonful of jam is absolutely scrumptious stirred into plain, whole-milk yogurt. Ice cream truly shines when kissed with nuts, herbs, fresh and dried fruits, extracts, and liquors. Let your imagination hold court when deciding how to jazz up homemade dairy items.

CALCIUM CHLORIDE

Unless you own your own milking animal or otherwise have access to raw milk, the milk used in your home dairy-making will be purchased from your local grocer, which means that it will be homogenized and pasteurized. These processes can interfere with the calcium

ASH

Historically, the ash used in cheese-making came from an actual fire. These days, the ash more likely is sourced from salt and vegetables that are dried and powdered. The ash serves a number of different functions. It creates a hospitable environment for surface mold growth, desirable in certain cheeses. Adding ash, an alkaline

substance, works to neutralize the acidity found in cheese, which might otherwise slow down ripening and, consequently, flavor development. Ash also provides a bit of visual interest, providing a darkened contrast to the paleness of the cheese. Also known as activated charcoal, ash can be purchased from cheese-making suppliers as well as drugstores.

KEFIR GRAINS

Kefir (a fermented beverage we'll discuss at greater length in chapter 5, Cultured Dairy) can be made from either a starter culture or from "live grains." The grains, looking a bit like cauliflower florets, are a jellylike community of bacteria and yeasts mixed with proteins, lipids, and

sugars (yum, right?). The grains can't be made, but must be obtained from actively fermenting kefir. You can purchase kefir grains, or look for someone making kefir nearby who might be able to part with some.

Portrait of a Cheese-maker

Jeff and Claudia

Some people manage to skillfully pursue multiple career paths in one lifetime. There's the doctor who gives up medicine to become a goat farmer or the stay-at-home mom who returns to college and goes on to become Secretary of State. Then there are the people who live both lives simultaneously. Claudia is one of those people. By day, she serves as director of operations at the Rock 'n' Roll Camp for Girls. During off hours, she runs Urban Cheesecraft, a cheesemaking kit and supply company, along with her partner Jeff.

Claudia got hooked on all things cheese after trying her hand at paneer-making while working at an Indian restaurant in high school. Curious about skills lost or overrun in the pursuit of mass production and convenience, she looked to her background of helping her grandmother cook, and the result was Urban Cheesecraft. Explaining her love of the craft, Claudia states, "I love cheese first and foremost, but I also love the self-sufficiency and empowerment I feel when I take a humble gallon of milk and create something entirely different. It's part meditation, part art, part science, and part magic for me—full of surprises. It fills me with awe, peace, and joy! Honestly!"

When not helping young girls find their inner Joan Jett, Claudia and Jeff spend a bit of time every week crafting fresh cheeses from cow's and goat's milk. Their homemade dairy roster includes mozzarella, queso blanco, ricotta, and chèvre. Urban Cheesecraft kits include molds, equipment, ingredients, and instructions for helping fledgling cheese-makers get started. Inspiring rock stars and dairy-makers alike, Claudia proves that it's possible to both eat your cheese and make it, too!

Chapter 3
Equipment:
Creamery Necessities

As with any new venture, a few tools specific to the task will be in order. Fortunately, for home dairy-making, many of those essential items are most likely already hanging out in your kitchen. Many of you will find it surprisingly easy to get started culturing yogurt and churning out butter. Once you've assembled the necessary equipment, crafting cream cheese for your morning bagel, mozzarella for a pizza dinner, or vanilla ice cream for that birthday party will be a breeze. In fact, you might just wonder why you didn't join in on the DIY dairy adventure sooner!

There's a great deal of overlap in the tools and materials used in home dairy-making. Equipment used in making cheese will also be used in making yogurt, and so on. I'll detail all of the basic gear you'll need on hand first, then walk you through those items specific to creating certain products. Depending on your budget, time constraints, and personal preferences you might choose to substitute cleverly appropriated everyday items for costly specialized equipment and tools (check out pages 55, 87, and 100 for DIY options). Everyone's needs are different, so when the time comes to start your own homemade dairy adventure, read through a recipe first, consider all of your equipment options, and then choose what feels best for you.

ESSENTIAL SUPPLIES

The following items are the go-to tools you'll visit, revisit, and then visit once more whenever you make homemade dairy products. Most likely, you've already got these objects on hand. For those you lack, a quick trip to the nearest kitchen supply store or online dairy-making supplier will get you suited up in no time.

Cheesecloth and Butter Muslin

You'll find these cloths to be indispensable in your home-dairy tool kit. Cheesecloth, as its name implies, was originally used to wrap cheeses for preserving. While still used for this purpose, it is more routinely used to drain whey from curds and for lining cheese molds intended for hard cheeses. The loose-woven fabric doesn't shed any fibers or lint into curds and won't retain flavors. Butter muslin is similar in use to cheesecloth, yet quite different in structure, possessing a finer, tighter weave.

In order for it to hold up to the rigors of regular home dairy-making, be sure to start with good quality cheesecloth right out of the gate. While you might be tempted to opt for the packaged variety available in grocery stores, I urge you, buyer beware! Such offerings are flimsy and shabbily made, not to mention possessed of holes large enough for smaller curds to slide right through. Source quality cheesecloth and butter muslin from a dairy-product supplier. Fortunately, it can withstand repeated use with proper cleaning.

To sanitize cheesecloth or butter muslin, boil a pot of water, add the soiled cheesecloth or butter muslin, and boil for two minutes. Remove the pot from the heat, drain off the water, and rinse the cheesecloth in cold water until all food debris is removed. Wring it out thoroughly and allow to air dry.

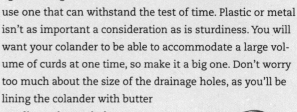

Colander

You'll return to your colander again and again, so be sure to use one that can withstand the test of time. Plastic or metal isn't as important a consideration as is sturdiness. You will want your colander to be able to accommodate a large volume of curds at one time, so make it a big one. Don't worry too much about the size of the drainage holes, as you'll be lining the colander with butter muslin or cheesecloth.

Dairy Thermometer

Because reaching or holding specific temperatures is crucial to many home dairy processes—a few degrees variation can render curds into completely different products—a reliable thermometer will be necessary. Dairy thermometers range from 0 to 220°F (104°C) and show 2-degree increments. Whichever style you choose, it must have a stem at least 2 inches long in order to reach into the milk and produce an accurate reading. In my experience, and in researching feedback from others, I've found a digital thermometer with a stainless-steel clip-on and a built-in timer to be the best option. Setting the timer to sound when the desired temperature has been achieved frees you up to do other things while your milk warms. Besides, we all know a watched pot never boils.

Double Boiler

Basically just another way of saying "a pot inside a pot," a double boiler is useful when you need to warm milk gradually and evenly. It needn't be anything fancy. If you'd rather not purchase a dedicated double boiler set, a double boiler can be fashioned by putting a smaller stockpot into a larger one to which 1 to 1½ inches of water has been added. Make certain the bottom of the mixing bowl doesn't come in contact with the water, otherwise the bowl's contents will overheat, defeating all of your efforts.

Glass Jar and Lid

When making yogurt and butter, you will need a glass Mason or canning jar, along with a lid. For yogurt, the glass jar is simply the vessel that will hold the mixture as it warms and cultures. In the case of butter-making, the "shaken jar" method is a low-tech, calorie-burning means of rendering cream into butter. While a variety of jar sizes are available, those most often used in butter and yogurt-making are half-pint, pint, and quart.

Saucepan

You will need a medium, heavy-bottomed stainless-steel pot for warming up milk for making yogurt, ice cream, and some soft cheeses. Ideally, it should hold up to 1 gallon of milk. Be sure to use only stainless-steel or chip-free enameled pots, as the acids present in milk can interact with aluminum, drawing the metal out of the pot and into the milk.

Measuring Cups

A glass measuring cup with a pouring spout is best. I like to have two sizes available: 8 ounces and 64 ounces is ideal. It is recommended that your equipment be completely sterile each time you fire up the home dairy. This is easier to achieve, in my experience, with glass equipment, as plastic can become scratched and retain residues, rendering it susceptible to contamination.

Sieve

A sturdy sieve will be needed in certain dairy-making processes, such as straining buttermilk off of butter and straining custard when making ice cream. Choose a medium version, as anything too small will just be a nuisance and an especially large sieve can be cumbersome.

Measuring Spoons

Keep a sturdy set of metal measuring spoons on hand. I've found them to be less susceptible to breakage than the plastic variety, unlikely to melt if they get too close to the stove, and less likely to become scratched, thereby making them more difficult to properly clean and sterilize.

Skimmer or Perforated Ladle

Your skimmer will be one of the tools you reach for most when making homemade dairy goods, especially in cheese-making. Utterly indispensable for transferring curds from the pot into the colander for draining, its large, flat diameter allows for easy lifting without breaking up curds. Stick with stainless steel, as it offers greater durability and assurance of sanitization than that offered by plastic utensils.

Long-handled Metal Spoon

A long spoon is helpful for stirring and combining liquids. Again, metal is advisable, as plastic and wood can absorb flavors and residues, posing risks for contamination. If you're going to spend time, attention, and money on making homemade dairy products, you don't want opportunistic bacteria to spread all over your lovingly prepared goods on account of a cheap utensil.

String or Twine

Some dairy products will need to be swaddled in cheesecloth or butter muslin and suspended to allow the whey to drip off. That's where string comes into play.

Any kitchen string or butcher's twine will work here. You can also get creative and use craft twine or even strong raffia in a pinch. Whatever you choose, just make sure it's sturdy. Should a phone call, unexpected house guest, or other need draw you out of the kitchen, few things might make you cry into your curds and whey more than a poorly secured bundle of dairy deliciousness, plunged to an untimely demise all over your kitchen floor.

CHEESE TOOLS

The type of cheese you are making factors heavily into the type of equipment you will need to make it. For example, a cheese press will only come into play when making hard cheeses. If you opt to jump completely into the dairy vat, as it were, read up on all types of equipment and then make your purchases (or make the equipment yourself) accordingly.

Cheeseboard

Not to be confused with marble or granite boards used for serving finished cheeses, this type of cheeseboard is an integral component to the aging process. It is basically a cutting board, used here as a drying platform. Cheeseboards are also used in aging and, when needed, as drainage stands for certain cheeses. Either plastic or wood cheeseboards are both acceptable for use, so long as fastidious cleaning hygiene is practiced. If you decide to use a wooden board, seek out one made of birch, maple, or bamboo, as the tannins in cherry and oak can be harmful to your cheese, potentially imbuing it with a bitter, astringent taste.

Cheese Trier

This device is what allows cheese-makers to sample a bit of cheese from the center of a wheel to test for ripeness. Made of stainless steel and used only when making hard cheeses, the trier lets a cheese-maker check on where their cheese is in its aging process without having to cut a wedge out of the wheel itself. The trier removes a core of cheese (similar to the core removed by an apple corer); a bit of the core is sampled and then the remaining portion is repositioned in the hole, allowing the aging process to continue.

Cheese Press

A cheese press is needed when making hard cheeses. Presses work by applying continued pressure onto curds that have been placed into a mold. The pressure squeezes whey from the curds, forming them into a solid mass. You can purchase a cheese press or make your own (see page 100 for DIY plans). Either way, your press should be easy to put together and take apart, making the process easy from start to clean-up.

Cheese Molds

Molds are used for forming curds into specific shapes. They are used in the final stages of cheese-making and determine the ultimate shape of your cheese. From rounds to pyramids, columns to hearts, cheese molds come in a variety of shapes and sizes. Commercially purchased cheese molds are made from wood, stainless steel, ceramic, and food-grade plastic. It is also possible to make your own molds from appropriated containers. See "Bend Me, Shape Me, Anyway You Want Me" on page 87 for DIY cheese mold options.

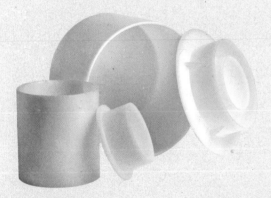

Cheese Followers

Used primarily when making hard cheeses, followers are flat disks of wood or plastic that sit snugly atop cheese molds. Without them, cheese curds would spill and seep out when subjected to the rigors of pressing. As pressure is applied, followers sink into the cheese mold, compressing the cheese in the process.

Cheese Wax

This type of wax is made especially for use in cheese-making and is deliberately soft and pliant. Used to keep hard cheeses from drying out during aging, wax also keeps harmful bacteria out of cheese while it is ripening. You may want to devote a used or worn-out pot expressly to cheese waxing, as attempting to remove the hardened wax can be a colossal challenge.

Curd Knife

You'll need a long knife, at least 10 inches in length, for cutting curds in some cheese-making recipes. The knife should be able to reach the bottom of the pot containing the curds without its handle touching the curds. It should also be relatively thin and capable of cutting straight lines. If you lack a curd or "cheese-cutting" knife such as those sold by cheese-making suppliers, a long, flat kitchen knife or cake spatula may be used.

Drip Tray

A drip tray is simply the container into which whey will drain during cheese pressing, keeping whey from running all over your countertops. Most commercially made cheese presses will come with their own tray. Should yours break, it can be replaced with an aluminum pie plate.

Drying Mats

Similar in use to cheeseboards, drying mats are made of bamboo or food-grade plastic. Mats can be purchased from cheese-making suppliers, Asian supermarkets (sushi mats), or craft supply stores (food-grade plastic in varying sizes). Drying mats are necessary for draining cheeses such as Brie, Camembert, and Coulommiers and also aid in the aging and air-drying process following pressing.

Spray Bottle

This is used in making mold-ripened cheeses. A light mist of mold solution is sprayed over the surface of the cheese, providing just the right amount of inoculant to get things ripening properly. Care must be taken not to over-mist, as doing so can turn a little bit of mold into a nasty beast. To prevent cross-contamination, each type of mold or bacteria will need its own spray bottle. To keep things sanitary, use only newly purchased bottles as opposed to repurposing a spray bottle you currently own.

Ripening Refrigerator

A number of hard cheeses need to age, some for a handful of days, weeks, or months, and some even for years. While aging, the temperature and relative humidity in the aging environment must be carefully maintained in order for proper acidity to develop, as well as to control mold growth. If you have a basement whose temperature never goes over 68°F (20°C), then you've got the equivalent of a cheese cave. If your basement is too warm or nonexistent, a dedicated, dormitory-sized refrigerator can do the job. Put a bowl of water in the bottom, set the temperature to 55°F (13°C), add your cheese, and, presto, consider yourself the proud owner of a modern-day cheese cave!

Stockpot

A large stainless-steel stockpot will be one of your most frequently used items in home dairy-making. Anything holding between 1 and 4 gallons of milk will work, depending on the size of your family and the frequency with which you consume dairy products (my house of two can put back a lot of dairy). An unchipped enamel pot works equally well.

BUTTER TOOLS

Making homemade butter is really quite simple. It can be as high or low-tech as you'd like it to be. If you'd like to streamline the necessary equipment, simply use your muscles to shake the cream into whipped submission. Otherwise, a food processor takes care of the work in short order.

Butter Churn or Food Processor

There are a number of different means of creating homemade butter. An electric churn makes butter from cream in about 30 minutes and involves no greater effort than pouring the cream into a large glass jar. A motor rests atop the jar and, once switched on, a plunger (also known as a "paddle" or "dasher") agitates the cream, separating water molecules from oil molecules. The resultant liquid is buttermilk, and the solid substance is butter. An electric model can be a great investment if you plan to make large quantities of butter on a regular basis. These can be expensive, though, so I'd suggest purchasing one only if you intend to sell your butter or otherwise market it.

A hand-cranked churn produces the same result as the motorized version, only with a little more elbow grease. Cream is poured into a glass jar and then whipped via a crank secured onto the lid of the jar. Less costly than electric models, its only drawback (if perceived as such) is its need for physical labor. Otherwise, it's an electricity-free way to make butter and, perhaps, give a task to squirmy children.

Asked to conjure up images of butter churns, likely an old-fashioned dasher-style churn will comes to mind. A small, tapered barrel holds a dasher that is moved up and down repeatedly to make butter. Not ideal for regular use, they can be difficult to clean and are susceptible to leaking. Antique dashers are more often kept as collector's items than for actual butter-making these days.

Finally, butter-making can also be accomplished with the help of a food processor. Although many home cooks may already possess a food processor, it is absolutely optional when making butter, although it can certainly expedite the process.

Butter Molds

A variety of molds exist for fashioning butter into all sorts of whimsical shapes, from stars, to hearts, to pineapples. I'm a fan of the asterisk/swirl myself. Made from plastic, food-grade silicone, or wood, butter molds are perfect tools for those times when gussying up your butter is in order.

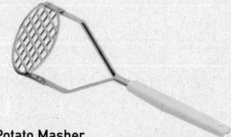

Potato Masher

A potato masher (or even simply two forks) is helpful when making butter by hand (i.e., without a machine). It needn't be fancy, requiring only a handle that will permit comfortable repeated kneading.

ICE CREAM & YOGURT TOOLS

While making yogurt or ice cream at home might never have occurred to you before, it should. It's easily done with the right equipment. As with other dairy-making endeavors, making yogurt or ice cream can involve repurposing basic equipment you already have, or acquiring specialty equipment suited expressly to the task at hand.

Hand-crank Ice Cream Churn

These are the ice cream machines our forefathers (and foremothers) used, cranking and churning out frozen delicacies with the aid of ice, rock salt, and good old-fashioned elbow grease. In this configuration, the cream mixture goes into an inner bowl, which is placed inside the larger churn. A layered mixture of ice and rock salt is then sandwiched between the cream-containing bowl and the interior wall of the churn. Salt causes the ice to melt more quickly and water to freeze faster. A paddle inside the inner bowl is activated when the hand crank atop the churn is turned. As the salt begins to melt the ice, heat generated by the paddling action is pulled out of the cream mixture and into the salt and ice mixture, freezing the cream. Depending on the model and manufacturer, and the size of the churn, a hand-crank model can be less expensive than an electric ice cream maker. However, it can also become rather messy, as the melting ice creates a pool of salty water that must be disposed of and replaced before a fresh batch can be made.

Electric Ice Cream Maker

These can be immensely handy for those pressed for time or short on hand-cranking labor. I love mine and use it all summer long. An electric ice cream maker operates with little assistance outside of plugging it in, filling the bowl, and turning the switch on. A little bit of advance planning is required, however. A double-walled bowl containing a solution capable of freezing below the freezing point of water must be frozen in a regular kitchen freezer for 24 hours before you begin. After the pre-freeze period, the bowl is placed inside the machine cavity, the cream mixture is poured in, the machine is turned on, and an interior paddle begins to churn the concoction. The cream begins to freeze as it makes contact with the frozen bowl, and, about 20 or so minutes later, the ice cream is frozen. I plan ahead for ice-cream urges by leaving the double-walled bowl in the freezer at all times, ready to receive a creamy mixture should the mood strike.

Electric Yogurt Maker

These machines regulate the temperature during your yogurt's incubation. This can be especially handy if your house temperature is too variable, you don't have the right setup for keeping the temperature consistent, or you don't want to be bothered with babysitting your yogurt (although it's a pretty docile ward, as far as caretaking responsibilities go). Otherwise, a number of means exist for incubating yogurt without use of a yogurt maker. See the sidebar on page 55 for suggestions on rigging up your own incubating device.

Chapter 4

Butter & Ghee:
Butter Me Up!

Butter, in my opinion, is downright swoon-worthy. It possesses a flavor so divine, a mouthfeel so rich and creamy, an aroma so promising of scrumptiousness that I've yet to meet a pat of butter I didn't like. Whether it's found in flaky piecrusts or melted into rich hollandaise and béarnaise sauces, slathered on hot biscuits or drizzled on straight-out-of-the-tandoori-oven naan, butter has captivated and transfixed taste buds the world over.

Now it's time to whip up this homemade dairy delight yourself, delivering butter's timeless tastiness to those gathered 'round your table. For those of you into homemade gifting, never underestimate the power of festooning friends and loved ones with butter (so long as your recipient lives nearby). I can all but guarantee that a multitude of doors will be opened up when fresh, creamy, whipped-with-love butter is offered.

FARM WIVES & FACTORIES

Butter has been consumed with delicious enthusiasm by humans for millennia. Derived from the Greek word *bou-tyron*, (loosely translated as "cow cheese" from *bous* "ox or cow" and *tyros* "cheese"), butter use has been documented as far back as 2000 B.C. From India to Norway, Japan to Britain, and many points in between, butter now makes its appearance on the global dining table.

Historically the work of farmers' wives and milkmaids, butter was once formed by hand-agitating cream via a plunger or dasher-style churn. If it was to be consumed shortly, the butter would be pressed into molds resembling sheaves of wheat or other decorative motifs. Otherwise, it was stored in wooden or ceramic tubs that could be taken to the local mercantile store for sale or bartering. Surplus butter was also stored in wooden casks called "firkins." Just prior to being shipped, small holes were made into the top of the firkins and salty brine was added to fill any airspace remaining between the butter and the cask. The brine acted as a preservative; butter stored this way could be stored in perfect condition for several months.

The production of butter began making the move from farm to factory during the late 19th century. In the traditional butter-making process, cream is allowed to naturally separate from milk, floating to the top in a thick layer, and fermenting, or "ripening," slightly. The ripening imbues the finished butter with a more complex flavor profile. This method of cream extraction, like many time-honored traditions, can take a while. For those looking to produce butter on a large scale, it was a costly, lengthy, yet necessary step.

Enter Swedish engineer Carl Gustaf Patrik de Laval, inventor of the centrifugal cream separator. This device enabled cream to be extracted from milk much more expediently. The first cream centrifuges were expensive, cumbersome contraptions, so farms shipped their milk whole to factories, which separated the cream there. Over time, advances were made in the size and cost of the separators, permitting farmers to swiftly extract cream in the comfort of their own farm-based creameries. This cream is then shipped out to factories, which transform it into butter in giant mechanical churns.

NUTRITIOUS & DELICIOUS

By definition, butter is an emulsion of butterfat, water, air, and possibly salt. A foodstuff composed almost entirely of cream—no wonder so many people love it, right? When cream is churned or otherwise seriously agitated, granules of butterfat glob together and separate from the whey, now known as buttermilk. The butterfat is then washed with water and kneaded until all excess liquid is removed. In commercial creameries, cream is churned with huge revolving blades at a very high speed, quickly forming butterfat that, in turn, is then mechanically kneaded. In home butter making, however, the churning and kneading are achieved through old-fashioned elbow grease.

Butter, as you may well have guessed, is rather high in fat. In fact, it's made almost entirely of milk fat: 80 to 86 percent, depending on the diet of the animal from which it was sourced. As far as nutrients go, butter contains protein, calcium, phosphorus, potassium, and vitamins A, D, and E. On a chemical level, butter consists of a mixture of triglycerides, or fatty acids, that form a bond. Melting at just below body temperature, somewhere between 90 and 95°F (32 and 35°C), butter can be spread easily at room temperature.

Old-fashioned butter churns

HOT 'N' BUTTERED

A somewhat fickle fat, once the short-chain fatty acids in butter are heated, its structure completely changes. So, let's say you're making a cookie dough and want to warm up some butter in the microwave to make it easier to cream with the sugar. Oops, you overheat it, resulting in a runny soup. Even if you put the melted butter back in the refrigerator and re-solidify it, its structure will never return to its original form, as its emulsion has been broken. This structural change will, in turn, affect just how well your cookie dough performs (word for the wise—not well at all!).

Cooking with butter also requires care. The milk solids in butter will burn at a pretty low temperature, around 250°F (121°C), making it fairly easy to scorch your butter over high heat. If you want to heat butter over high temperatures without scorching, you need to clarify it first. Clarifying butter involves melting it over a low temperature until the butterfat and milk solids form separate camps in your pan. Pour off the milk solids, and the remaining butterfat can be placed over high heat and won't burn. Clarifying butter does affect butter's taste, as many of its characteristic flavor elements reside in the milk solids.

Carotene contributes to the yellow hue in butter.

COLOR THEORY

You may have wondered about the color of butter. Cow's milk is white, right? So, what's up with the yellow in butter? The greatest reason for the presence of a yellow hue in butter is carotene. Carotene is the vegetable form of vitamin A, which shows up not just in carrots, sweet potatoes, and cantaloupe, but also in grass. Butter made from the milk of cows that are allowed to pasture will have a greater degree of yellowish hue than from those fed on grain. The color will vary during times of the year when weather prevents cows from grazing or when grass is not growing in abundance. You can even see such seasonal variation in the milk of grass-fed cows, with more yellow milk in spring and summer and lighter toned milk during other times of the year.

That's not to say that grain-fed cows don't also possess carotene in their butterfat; they do, only not as much. Because many people have become accustomed to yellow-hued butter (without really knowing why), a bit of annatto is often added to commercially produced butter. A natural coloring, annatto is produced from the reddish-tinted pulp that surrounds seeds of achiote tree fruit. Used to color everything from cheese to margarine and even lipstick, the inclusion of annatto mimics the yellow that would be found in summer milk from grass-fed cows.

STORING BUTTER

There are a number of different ways to keep your butter fresh and tasty—whether store-bought or homemade. If you make a large batch, you might even want to divide it into portions and employ several storage options at once. The addition of salt to homemade butter is entirely optional and mostly a matter of taste, although salted butter remains fresh a bit longer than unsalted butter.

Fresh

The best means I've found for storing butter at room temperature (ideal for spreadability!) is to employ the use of a butter crock. Developed long before the existence of refrigerators, butter crocks (also known as "French" or "Acadian" butter dishes) are simply two-piece earthenware containers. The lid of the crock has an interior bowl into which butter is packed. This lid is

A butter crock

Portrait of a Butter-maker

Heather

Professionally trained as a chef, Heather spends her days working in higher education. Evenings, nights, and weekends, however, she can be found writing about food, developing recipes, and teaching private cooking classes. Several years ago, Heather made a commitment to convert her family to a more sustainable lifestyle. That transition began by eating foods locally and seasonally, and segued into planting a family vegetable garden, baking bread on a regular basis, and making homemade dairy products.

Although she didn't grow up with a family that regularly made their own dairy items (fond recollections of an ice cream-making aunt notwithstanding!), Heather recently began experimenting with making her own butter, as well as a bit of ice cream and cheese. She now makes butter twice monthly year-round, along with ice cream during the warmer months. When it comes to home dairy-making, Heather reinforces the culinary mantra that fresh is best: **"Always start with the freshest ingredients that you can find. The better the cream, eggs, sugar, herbs, etc., the better the final product will be."**

then inverted and placed inside the bottom bowl, into which cold water has been added. The water forms an airtight seal, preserving the butter by keeping it safe from bacteria in the air, while simultaneously holding the butter at room temperature. I've found that being fastidious about keeping crumbs out of the crock and changing out the water every two days keeps the butter fresh for about a week without spoilage. Sweet cream and cultured butter work equally well in a butter crock, so long as you are certain to keep it filled with cold water and consume the butter relatively quickly (never an issue in my house!).

Storage vessels for fresh butter

Chilled

If you intend to refrigerate your homemade butter until ready for use, it's best to wrap it up or store it in an airtight container. Butter begins to deteriorate

Wrap butter in parchment or waxed paper for long-term storage.

when exposed to air, so securing it tightly is paramount. Wax or parchment paper are perfect for wrapping, while lidded glass containers keep butter fresh without imparting any residual food flavors or aromas that can sometimes show up in plastic containers. Butter stored in the refrigerator will last for four months, if held at temperatures between 32 and 38°F (0 and 3°C). Personally, I've found butter to taste considerably fresher if consumed within two months and butter made from raw milk to taste best if refrigerated for no longer one month.

Frozen

If you have butter you'd like to freeze, you'll need to wrap it up or store it in an airtight container, much like refrigerator-bound butter. If you opt to wrap, I'd suggest you then slide it into an airtight freezer bag, to offer further protection against the formation of ice crystals. Frozen butter, if held at temperatures between -10 and -20°F (-23 and -28°C), will keep for up to one year. Its flavor will be best if used within six to eight months.

Butter Recipes

A number of different means of making butter at home exist. Depending on the type of equipment you own, and the flavor profile you prefer, it's possible to create butter manually, mechanically, or in a European "cultured" style, all from your kitchen. How cool is that? I have to warn you: The flavor of homemade butter is incomparable. When I first began making butter, I found myself daydreaming about it when doing something totally unrelated, such as folding laundry or planting my fall garden. Simply put, it's delicious. You'll wonder why you hadn't treated yourself to homemade butter much, much sooner!

Whipped Butter

For modern households, the mixer and food processor take on the responsibilities previously held by dashers, plungers, and barrel churns. Delicious butter can be yours in a fraction of the time provided by other means (although you won't get the same champion butter-making biceps you might have otherwise acquired).

Yield: Approximately 1 cup

YOU WILL NEED:

1 pint heavy cream

¼ teaspoon salt, optional

Food processor or stand mixer

TO PREPARE:

1. Allow the cream to come to room temperature, right around 72 to 74°F (22 to 23°C). To do this, simply take the cream out of the refrigerator, set it on the counter, put a dairy thermometer into it, and check on it every 30 minutes or so until the temperature rises. This allows the cream to ripen and raises its acidity slightly, making it easier to whip and full of flavor.

2. Place the cream inside either a food processor or mixer bowl, and begin operating at medium speed. Turn the machine to high and process the cream through the butter-forming stages: first sloshy, then stiff, then finally dividing ranks and forming separately into butter and buttermilk. Depending on your machine, this could take between six and nine minutes (I average around eight minutes using a food processor).

3. Using a spatula, remove the butter from the machine, draining off the buttermilk. Place the butter in a medium bowl.

4. Run cold water over the butter. Empty the water out, and repeat several times until the water is clear in the bowl. Strain off any remaining water. If using salt, stir it in with a metal spoon.

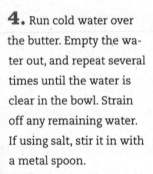

5. Place the butter on a cutting board. Using either clean hands, a wooden spoon, plastic pastry scraper, or a potato masher, begin pressing the butter repeatedly, allowing any liquid inside of it to drain off. Continue pressing until you no longer see liquid coming from your butter.

6. Depending on whether you intend to use your butter now or in the future, you can store it at room temperature in a butter crock, or chilled or frozen in wax or parchment paper, or a covered container in the refrigerator or the freezer.

Shake, Rattle & Roll

It is entirely possible to make butter simply by shaking a jar of cream. Take turns passing the jar to helping hands around the house (including children), shake it while listening to your favorite radio program, agitate it as you play fetch with your dog—whatever it takes to make the time pass and the cream transform. When making butter, I like to hold on to all of the heavenly buttermilk that oozes out of the creamy mass during straining and pressing. Perfect for biscuits and cornbread, it also works well in waffles and pancakes. *Yield: Approximately 1 cup*

TO PREPARE:

1. Allow the cream to come to room temperature, right around 72 to 74°F (22 to 23°C). To do this, simply take the cream out of the refrigerator, set it on the counter, put a dairy thermometer into it, and check on it every 30 minutes or so until the temperature rises. This allows the cream to ripen and raises its acidity slightly, making it easier to whip and full of flavor.

2. Place the cream and the marble inside your jar, secure the lid tightly, and begin shaking vigorously. Continue shaking, about once per second, until the cream begins to thicken. You'll hear it, as it changes from a constant sloshing sound to a heavier thud. This process will take anywhere between five and 30 minutes, depending on the intensity and frequency of the shaking.

3. Using a spatula, remove the butter from the jar, draining off the buttermilk. Take the marble out, and place the butter in a medium bowl. Finish the butter following steps 4 through 6 on page 44, and store as desired.

YOU WILL NEED:	
1	quart-sized jar with lid
1	pint heavy cream
1	glass marble
¼	teaspoon salt, optional

Cultured Butter

Cultured butter has a rich, mildly tangy flavor, and is far more common in Europe than in the United States, where sweet cream butter is preferred. This type of butter is made from fermented cream or cream that has had bacterial cultures added to it. During fermentation, bacteria present in the milk and air transform lactose (milk sugar) into lactic acid. This produces a product higher in butterfat than sweet cream butter (around 85 percent to sweet cream butter's 80 percent), providing a richer and, arguably, fuller butter flavor. Cultured butter purchased in stores is most often made with added *Lactococcus* and *Leuconostoc* bacteria. Homemade cultured butter is allowed to ferment naturally. **Yield: Approximately 1 cup**

YOU WILL NEED:

1 pint heavy cream

3 tablespoons plain whole milk yogurt, sour cream, or crème fraîche

¼ teaspoon salt, optional

Food processor or stand mixer

TO PREPARE:

1. Combine the cream and yogurt in a glass or ceramic bowl. Using a metal spoon, slowly and gradually incorporate the two until well mixed. Sealing the top with either plastic wrap or a plate large enough to cover the top of the bowl, let the mixture sit at a warm room temperature (75°F [24°C] is ideal) for 12 hours.

2. Place the fermented cream in a food processor or mixer bowl, and begin operating at medium speed. Turn the machine to high and process the cream through the butter-forming stages: first sloshy, then stiff, then finally dividing ranks and forming separately into butter and buttermilk. Depending on your machine, this could take between six and nine minutes.

3. Using a spatula, remove the butter from the machine, draining off the buttermilk. Place the butter in a medium bowl. Finish the butter following steps 4 through 6 on page 44, and store as desired.

Oh Ghee, Oh My

A type of clarified butter, ghee is widely used in Indian cooking. It is formed by simmering unsalted butter until its water cooks away and three layers form: whey protein, liquid fat, and casein. Simply strain the clarified fat out from the whey protein casein particles, and you have ghee. Because the substances that would otherwise promote rancidity have been removed (the casein particles and water, and their attendant microbes and enzymes), ghee can remain without refrigeration for several months, so long as it is stored in an airtight container. It's important for ghee to remain free of moisture, so don't use a wet or moist spoon when extracting some from its container. Ghee is ideal for use in high-heat or deep-frying, as it will not scorch. *Yield: Slightly less than 2 cups*

Homemade Ghee Recipe

YOU WILL NEED:

2 cups unsalted butter

TO PREPARE:

1. Place the butter in a medium stainless-steel saucepan. Melt the butter, and bring to a boil over medium-high heat.

2. Once the butter begins boiling, reduce the heat to medium. Watch for a foam to appear on the surface of the melted butter. After the foam disappears, watch for a second foam to form and for the butter to turn a darker, golden color. At this point, you should be able to see brown particles (milk solids) on the bottom of the pan and detect a popcornish scent.

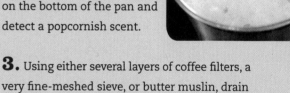

3. Using either several layers of coffee filters, a very fine-meshed sieve, or butter muslin, drain the mixture into a heatproof container. The strained liquid is clarified butter, or ghee.

4. Cover your container with a tight-fitting lid, and store out of direct sunlight at room temperature. Ghee solidifies when cool, but melts quickly when exposed to heat.

Compound Butters

Butter on its own is all well and good, but butter with flavorings added to it is transcendent! Butter can have any given number of helpful taste agents mixed in, creating what is called a "compound" or "composite" butter. Spices, herbs, liquors, dried fruits, powders— let your imagination go to town! Compound butters are delicious spread on bread, absolutely stellar atop hot vegetables or meats, and sweeter versions will make any dessert shine. The four variations below reflect a year's worth of seasonal offerings. Compound butter will keep in the freezer for up to two months. **Yield: *Slightly more than 1/2 cup***

YOU WILL NEED:

½ cup (1 stick) butter

Flavoring of your choice

TO PREPARE:

1. If you are beginning with chilled butter, it will first need to come to room temperature. Place it in a medium bowl for around 30 minutes to soften up.

2. If necessary, chop your flavorings finely and evenly. Combine with the butter and mash with a fork until well mixed.

3. Using a spatula, transfer your compound butter to a sheet of waxed paper. Wrapping the waxed paper around the butter, shape it into a cylinder approximately 6 to 8 inches long. Twist up each end of the waxed paper, as though it were a piece of candy, to secure the contents inside. Alternatively, place compound butter into individual butter molds.

4. Place the roll inside a plastic bag in the freezer and allow to firm up. Use as needed.

SEASONAL VARIATIONS

 SPRING

Lemon and Dill

This would be delicious spread onto steamed or pan-sautéed asparagus, spooned atop piping hot new potatoes, or dolloped onto grilled salmon. Add 1 tablespoon finely chopped fresh dill and the grated zest of 1 lemon.

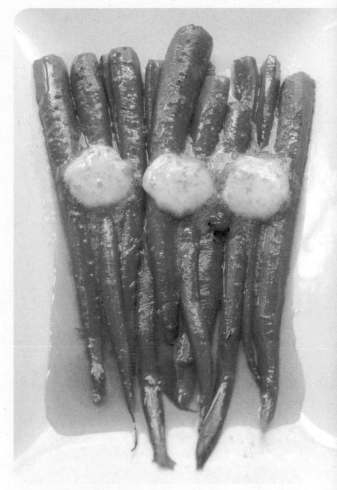

SUMMER

Herbal Bouquet

Try this compound butter spread liberally atop hot baguettes, tucked into mashed potatoes, or dolloped onto roasted root vegetables; you could also slice a coin onto a freshly seared steak. Finely chop 2 teaspoons each fresh marjoram, rosemary, thyme, tarragon, basil, and fresh or dried lavender buds. Mix the herbs with softened butter as described at left.

AUTUMN

Spice of Life

Tuck this butter into hot apple-walnut muffins, spread it on pumpkin pancakes, or add to straight-from-the-oven sweet potatoes. Yum! Mix together $1/2$ teaspoon ground cinnamon, $1/4$ teaspoon ground nutmeg, $1/4$ teaspoon ground cloves, and $1/4$ teaspoon allspice. Combine the spices with the softened butter.

WINTER

Triple Orange Compound Butter

This would be divine spread over hot waffles, nestled inside a poppy seed scone, or melted over glazed carrots. Combine 1 tablespoon orange juice, 2 teaspoons freshly grated orange zest, and $1^{1}/2$ tablespoons triple sec with the softened butter.

Browned Butter

Literally translated as "hazelnut butter," *beurre noisette* (browned butter) adds a nutty, complex dash of deliciousness to both sweet and savory dishes and is an essential component in classical French cooking. Creating browned butter is somewhat similar to making ghee, or clarified butter, except that the milk solids aren't strained out. As delicious in pastries and desserts as it is spooned over fish, chicken, eggs, or vegetables (think broccoli and brussels sprouts), browned butter will "butter you up" and leave you begging for seconds. *Yield: Slightly less than ¼ cup*

YOU WILL NEED:

4 tablespoons unsalted butter

TO PREPARE:

1. Create an ice-water bath by filling either the kitchen sink or a large metal bowl with cold water and a few ice cubes.

2. Place the butter in a medium stainless-steel saucepan. Melt, then bring to a boil over medium heat.

3. Once the butter begins boiling, monitor it closely. Stir continually, watching for the butter to turn a darker, golden, hazelnut-like color and a nutty, but not burned, smell.

4. Remove the saucepan from the heat, and dip the bottom into the waiting ice-water bath. This stops the browning process and prevents any continued in-pan cooking.

5. Serve immediately or store in a covered jar in the refrigerator and use within one week.

Variations: Browned butter possesses a seemingly infinite capacity for variation. Squeeze in the juice of half a lemon and 3 tablespoons chopped fresh parsley to create *beurre meunière*, perfect over fish, eggs, or steamed veggies. For a kiss of sweetness, add 1 tablespoon maple syrup and ¼ teaspoon ground nutmeg; serve over pancakes, waffles, or crepes.

Portrait of a Dairy Dabbler

Sarah

Sarah knows that home is where the heart is. As co-owner of Nest Organics (mom Truly makes up the other half), a retail store selling organic, pure, and sustainable products for the home and family, she's acutely aware of the benefits derived from living naturally. Her store is committed to engendering the purchase of conscientious home products that blend function, style, and sustainability.

Food is just as integral a component to a healthy home as are furnishings and garments. In her dedication to pursing a natural lifestyle for herself and her family of four, Sarah makes a number of her own dairy products. For over 13 years, she has made everything from paneer to ice cream to butter several times a week, based on the time of year and need. She's tried her hand at mascarpone and regularly makes buttermilk when baking. Her husband is also in on the dairy action, making yogurt for their family.

Her dairy-making horizon holds promise of homemade mozzarella and hard cheeses. Although she wasn't raised with a dairy-maker in the house, she's adapted to making home-based dairy products with ease. "Homemade dairy is so much more delicious than store-bought and pretty easy, so it seems silly not to make it!"

Chapter 5
Cultured Dairy:
Cultivated Tastes

From Greece to Germany, Australia to the Americas, cultured dairy products are integral parts of numerous food cultures. The puckery twang characteristic of these foods is only part of their appeal. Containing a veritable bounty of beneficial bacteria, cultured foods are both good to eat and good for you. The best part is how easy they are to make at home. Get ready to learn just how delicious it is to sample the world's cultures.

FERMENTING CHANGE

Cultured dairy products are, by definition, those that have undergone fermentation. Fermentation in foods is a result of the action of yeast and bacteria. Chemically, carbohydrates are transformed into alcohol and carbon dioxide (as well as other organic acids) in an anaerobic environment (one that is lacking oxygen).

As discussed in the recipe for cultured butter (page 46) in chapter 4, during fermentation, bacteria found in milk and air interact, turning milk sugar (lactose) into lactic acid. The bacteria responsible for this conversion can include *Streptococcus*, *Lactobacillus*, *Lactococcus*, and *Leuconostoc*. When exposed to temperatures around 90°F (32°C), these bacteria begin to proliferate very, very rapidly—as in, doubled-in-size-in-20-minutes rapidly.

The presence of these bacteria result in a number of features specific to fermented foods. The development of a characteristic "cultured" flavor is one such feature. Fermented dairy products also offer increased digestibility, as the proteins and sugars in the milk have already begun to break down, rendering them "predigested." For this reason many people who avoid drinking milk due to lactose-intolerance find that they have no problem digesting dairy products that have been cultured. There is also evidence that consumption of fermented dairy products may lower cholesterol, protect against bone loss, and bolster the immune system against illness.

CULTURAL STUDIES

Culturing dairy is nothing new. People have been fermenting dairy products for just about as long as they've been domesticating animals. You've got to do something with all that milk, right? Before the age of refrigeration, warm milk from animals was gathered and allowed to ferment, using the remains of previously cultured batches as the "starter." Common strains of *Streptococcus* and *Lactobacillus* did all the work, beating out the microbial competition in a bacterial smackdown. As a result, the milk was prevented from spoiling and could be stored for several days—or possibly even weeks—without refrigeration.

Kefir, buttermilk, and yogurt are all examples of cultured dairy products.

Various strains of culturing bacteria can now be prepared in the laboratory and are available commercially to the home dairy-maker, permitting a wide range of cultured dairy alchemy. In many of the recipes in this chapter, it is possible to use an existing batch of cultured dairy (either purchased or made at home) as your starter, such as yogurt you made or gathered up at the grocery store. Alternatively, you can use a purchased starter, available from dairy-making supply companies, to inoculate fresh milk and get the party started.

Yogurt

Spooned into granola, mixed with cucumber and spices for a cooling raita, or blended into a refreshing fruit shake, yogurt has a long and storied reputation as a cross-cultural palate-pleaser. Yogurt's pudding-like texture, coupled with an intense tanginess, makes it perfect for any meal, from breakfast to dinner (think chilled yogurt soup) to dessert. This cultured treat is a treasure trove of vitamins and minerals, containing generous amounts of iodine, calcium, phosphorus, potassium, zinc, pantothenic acid, and vitamins B_2 and B_{12}. It is also a great source of protein, with 8 ounces supplying around 8 grams.

Prior to the 20th century, yogurt was consumed primarily in the Middle East, Asia, Russia, and several eastern European countries. During the 1900s, research conducted by Dr. Ilya Mechnikov brought yogurt to the attention of the Western world. The Ukrainian-born doctor was given a Nobel prize for his work on the role of beneficial bacteria—now commonly known as probiotics—in digestion. Based on the dietary habits of some of the world's longest-lived individuals, such as inhabitants of eastern Europe, known for their regular consumption of cultured dairy foods, he theorized that lactic acid could prolong life, and consumed soured milk and yogurt daily. His research inspired a new generation of yogurt makers and eaters, introducing the puckery treat to the entire world.

Yogurt recipe

When you're just starting out, you have the option of using a packet of commercially prepared yogurt starter or a dollop of prepared yogurt, purchased from the market. If you decide to use prepared yogurt, make certain it indicates somewhere on the label that it possesses "live, active cultures." The existence of these cultures is absolutely crucial to the success of your batch. While you can use milk of any type, the higher the butterfat in your ingredients, the thicker and creamier the end product will be.

Yield: Slightly more than 4 cups; 5 half-pints, if jarred

YOU WILL NEED:

4 cups whole, low-fat, or skim milk

3 tablespoons live yogurt or 1 packet dried yogurt culture

If you prefer a thick, stick-your-spoon-in-and-it-remains-upright type of yogurt, add 4 tablespoons powdered dry milk or 1 tablespoon unflavored gelatin.

TO PREPARE:

1. If you are using a thickening agent, whisk the dried milk or gelatin into the milk until combined. Warm the milk gently in a medium saucepan over medium-high heat until it almost reaches the boiling point, right around 180°F (82°C).

2. Remove the milk from the heat and allow it to cool to 110 to 115°F (43 to 46°C). Using a metal spoon, stir in the yogurt or dried yogurt culture. Mix until well incorporated.

3. Transfer the mixture to whatever container you will be culturing it in, such as yogurt machine glass jars, Mason jars, lidded glass bowl, or a thermos.

4. Hold the yogurt at 110 to 115°F (43 to 46°C) for the next six hours. Consider any of the "Incubating Ideas" options as a way to maintain the necessary temperature for proper yogurt formation.

5. Store the yogurt in an airtight container in the refrigerator, and use within one to two weeks.

"Incubating Ideas": DIY Yogurt Makers

Try any one of these ideas for successfully regulating yogurt without the aid of an electric yogurt maker.

BLANKET

Preheat an oven to 120°F (49°C). Place the yogurt mixture in a glass or ceramic bowl, and cover with a lid or plate. Turn the oven off, and place the yogurt inside for six hours.

COOLER

Place the yogurt mixture into one (or several, depending on volume) glass jars. Place the jars in a small to medium insulated cooler overnight, along with several jars of hot water.

SLOW COOKER

Preheat a slow cooker on low. Add glass jars of yogurt to the pot. Turn off the heat, cover with a lid, and allow to incubate six hours or overnight.

SUN

Let the sun do all the cooking for you. Place your yogurt mixture in a ceramic or glass bowl, cover with a lid, and put in a spot that will be consistently sunny for four to six hours. During the dog days of summer, when the sun is seriously scorching, it might be wise to either start this means of incubating quite early in the morning (7-ish), or wait for a more hospitable, balmier day to make yogurt. This technique can be used year-round, as you'll be culturing your yogurt indoors, so long as the ambient room temperature remains between 68 and 74°F (20 and 23°C).

THERMOS

Simply fill an insulated thermos with your yogurt mixture, put the lid on, wrap a couple of kitchen towels around it, and put in an area away from drafts, such as a pantry or cabinet, for six hours or overnight. The ambient temperature should be somewhere between 68 and 74°F (20 and 23°C) for your yogurt to culture properly.

Buttermilk

My grandmother was absolutely wild about buttermilk. It was always in her refrigerator and, if pressed to choose, was probably her favorite beverage, bar none. Nanny's buttermilk was the store-bought kind, but making it at home couldn't be easier. In fact, when you make butter, you produce one type of buttermilk as a by-product, hence the original meaning of the term. This is considered "traditional" buttermilk. Store-bought buttermilk, or cultured buttermilk, is a fermented beverage, unrelated to butter-making.

Similar in flavor to yogurt, buttermilk's texture is thicker, coating the entire tongue. If cultured, or allowed to ferment like yogurt, buttermilk becomes imbued with lactic acid, giving it the telltale sour flavor. (Buttermilk that is simply the liquid left behind in making butter at home isn't cultured.) Commercially prepared buttermilk is made by adding bacterial culture to warmed milk and then holding the mixture at a low temperature for 12 to 15 hours. Homemade buttermilk will be made in the same manner, either by using remnants of the last batch of cultured buttermilk you created, or by inoculating milk with a buttermilk starter culture.

Buttermilk recipe

Once you get on board with using buttermilk, you'll find all sorts of opportunities to sneak it in. This recipe would be delicious served ice cold (my grandmother's preference), incorporated into biscuits (my preference), or rendered into an ice cream with some serious kick (everyone in the world's preference). Check the label and make sure that your starter buttermilk contains live, active cultures. **Yield: Slightly more than 4 cups**

YOU WILL NEED:

4 cups whole or skim milk

2/3 cup cultured buttermilk or 1 packet dried buttermilk culture

TO PREPARE:

1. Warm the milk gently in a medium saucepan over medium-high heat until it reaches 85°F (29°C).

2. Transfer the milk to a glass or ceramic container. Using a metal spoon or a wire whisk, stir in the buttermilk or dried buttermilk culture. Mix until well incorporated.

3. Cover the container with a plate or lid, and leave it at room temperature for 12 hours.

4. Store the buttermilk in an airtight container in the refrigerator and use within one to two weeks.

Portrait of a Dairy Renaissance Man

Patrick

Thriving at the intersection of "talk" and "walk," Patrick melds his many passions, interests, and disciplines into a life committed to conscientious living. A book and print designer by trade, Patrick, along with his life and business partner Holly, also runs the blog Veloculture (devoted to photographing stylish bicycle-riding), founded an all-volunteer egg co-op, and teaches beginner classes on chicken-keeping and cheese-making.

Although he's been making home dairy products for nearly a decade, it was involvement in a milk co-op that initiated a dairy-making interest in earnest. "We got a gallon of raw Jersey milk each week. This inspired quite a bit of home dairying, as you can well imagine, and got me started in making yogurt." Patrick finds the dairy products he makes at home to be of better quality and less expensive than store-bought substitutes. Some of his favorites are hard to find, so home-dairying is really the only option. To date, his repertoire includes paneer, ghee, crème fraîche, buttermilk (using both cow's and goat's milk), yogurt, yogurt cheese, and feta.

Patrick teaches his popular "Home Dairying 101" class through a program sponsored by his city, as well as at a nearby farm. It has been met with great success and he plans to continue it, tweaking it as he goes. As a seasoned dairy-maker, Patrick offers the following well-cultured advice: "Home dairying offers a lot of latitude, but it helps to follow recipes to the letter at first, so that you can understand how the process works."

Kefir

Whether you pronounce it *ka-fear*, *kef-ur*, or *key-fur* makes no difference. Similar in a number of ways to yogurt, kefir's difference lies in the bacteria it possesses. Kefir contains *Lactobacillus Caucasus*, *Acetobacter* species, and *Saccharomyces* (yeast), all known for their ability to penetrate the mucosal lining of the digestive tract. These microbes colonize the intestinal lining, giving the boot to harmful intruders potentially residing there. As a result, it becomes easier for your body to ward off pathogens like intestinal parasites and *E. coli*.

You can make kefir from any type of milk, including animal (cow, sheep, goat, what have you), coconut, rice, and soy. While the milk used can be variable, the invariable part of the recipe is kefir grains—a fascinating blend of bacteria and yeasts in a protein/lipid/sugar base. These grains look like cauliflower or white coral and can be as tiny as a grain of rice or as large as a human hand. The grains activate the fermentation process and are strained out before consumption. Kefir made at home is allowed to culture at ambient room temperature for up to a day. As it ferments, the kefir sours and becomes mildly carbonated, becoming very mildly alcoholic in the process (although you won't be getting drunk off of kefir, at levels of one to two percent!).

Kefir recipe #1 (Using Live Grains)

Many find kefir perfect completely unadorned, without any flavor additions. It is also delicious blended with fruit, nuts, spices, and fresh herbs. (Strawberries and vanilla bean flecks mixed into fresh kefir is a personal favorite). Kefir is also an ideal candidate for inclusion in corn bread, its puckery punch a perfect foil to corn's sweetness!
Yield: Slightly more than 3 cups

YOU WILL NEED:

3 cups whole, skim, or low-fat milk

4 tablespoons live kefir grains

TO PREPARE:

1. Place the milk in a glass or ceramic container, and add the kefir grains.

2. Stir the grains gently, cover the jar loosely with a kitchen cloth, and leave it at room temperature for 18 to 24 hours.

3. At the end of the culturing time, once the mixture begins to thicken up a bit, give the jar a gentle stir. Strain off the liquid through a sieve or small-holed colander, taking care not to press on the grains while straining.

4. Transfer the strained liquid to a clean glass jar with a lid, and store in the refrigerator for up to three weeks.

5. To store the grains for future use, do not rinse them after straining. Instead, gently place the still-moist grains in a clean, lidded jar, and store them in the refrigerator. When you are ready, follow recipe steps 1 through 4 to make a new batch. With each subsequent batch, the number of kefir grains will continue to multiply. You can either choose to share some kefir booty with friends and family, or store the grains in your refrigerator for future use.

Kefir recipe #2 (Using Dried Starter Culture)

Kefir made from powdered starter culture will be slightly less fermented than that made from live grains. It will possess all of the same health benefits, however. Kefir made from starter culture can be used to make successive batches up to six or seven times. After that, you'll need to make a fresh batch using a new packet of powdered culture. Kefir made from live grains can be used to start new batches pretty much indefinitely. *Yield: Slightly more than 1 gallon*

YOU WILL NEED:

1 gallon milk

1 packet dried kefir culture

TO PREPARE:

1. Warm the milk gently in a medium saucepan over medium-high heat until it reaches 85°F (29°C).

2. Transfer the milk to a glass or ceramic container. Using a metal spoon or wire whisk, stir in the dried culture. Mix until well incorporated.

3. Cover the container with a plate or lid, and leave it at room temperature for 12 hours.

4. Store the kefir in an airtight container in the refrigerator, and use within three weeks. Once you've made your first batch of kefir, you can use that kefir to make successive batches before a new packet of culture will be required. To make successive batches, simply follow the recipe as above, replacing the starter culture packet with 1 cup kefir.

Sour Cream

Thick, tangy, and creamy, sour cream is a cultured dairy hall of famer. You begin with cream, which is, really, where all good things begin. To cream you add a starter culture, you provide a bit of heat, and end up with a product of a tartly sublime nature. Appearing in various incarnations worldwide, sour cream makes cameos in dishes as varied as Russian blini and ranch dressing.

Sour cream is quite high in butterfat, averaging between 12 and 18 percent. It is particularly well suited to thickening soups and sauces or as an ingredient in a thick dip. Sour cream can be made at home either by the addition of a prepared cultured product (in this case buttermilk) or a purchased dried starter culture. I'd make a strong case for whipping up your own sour cream, as many store-bought varieties include additional thickening agents and acids to artificially mimic the characteristic lactic-acid-derived sourness.

Sour Cream recipe

From Hungarian goulash to seven-layer bean dip, sour cream crosses all cultural divides. Try it as a baked potato topper, to impart a tart touch to coffeecake, or as a means of tempering the fiery heat of enchiladas. *Yield: Slightly more than 1 cup*

YOU WILL NEED:

1 cup heavy cream

¼ cup buttermilk*

*You can also make sour cream using a packet of dried starter culture. Simply increase the milk to 4 cups and follow the recipe as written, substituting your packaged culture for the buttermilk.

TO PREPARE:

1. Warm the cream gently in a small saucepan over medium-high heat until it reaches 85°F (29°C).

2. Transfer the cream to a glass or ceramic container. Using a metal spoon, stir in the buttermilk or dried culture. Mix until well incorporated.

3. Cover the container with a plate or lid, and leave it at room temperature for 12 hours.

4. After the culturing time has passed, your cream should have noticeably thickened. Store the sour cream in an airtight container in the refrigerator, and use within one to two weeks.

Crème Fraîche

Similar in flavor to sour cream, crème fraîche (pronounced "krem fresh") is cultured heavy cream, French-style. Developed before the time of refrigeration, crème fraîche cultured itself, as it were. As raw, unpasteurized cream sat at ambient temperature in buckets awaiting transport to market, lactic acid cultures formed and mild fermentation began to occur. The resultant tangy, soured taste became an intrinsic component of the French culinary landscape—and the world is all the better for it, in my opinion. Pasteurized cream won't develop lactic acid in the same manner if left to sit at room temperature, as the viable cultures were killed off during the pasteurization process. It will need to have cultures introduced to it in order for fermentation to occur.

Exceptionally velvety, the high fat content of crème fraîche prevents it from curdling when added to hot sauces and soups, making it a favorite of professional and home chefs alike. The bacterial cultures found in this cultured dairy product, introduced via either buttermilk, sour cream, or dried starter cultures, impart both flavor and thickness. Crème fraîche will be almost runny once first made, but gains body and solidifies over time. Flowing and oozy or firm and substantive, crème fraîche holds its own in the pantheon of cultured dairy delights.

Crème Fraîche recipe

Its applications seemingly infinite, crème fraîche is exquisite incorporated into sauces for pork or chicken, whipped with a smidge of confectioner's sugar and dolloped over hot fruit crisps, or stirred into hot pasta with fresh herbs. *Yield: Slightly more than 1 cup*

YOU WILL NEED:

1 cup heavy cream

2 tablespoons buttermilk or sour cream*

*You can also make crème fraîche using a packet of dried starter culture. Simply increase from 1 cup heavy cream to 4 cups milk and follow the recipe as written, substituting your packaged culture for the buttermilk or yogurt.

TO PREPARE:

1. Warm the cream gently in a small saucepan over medium-high heat until it reaches 85°F (29°C).

2. Transfer the cream to a glass or ceramic container. Using a metal spoon, stir in buttermilk, sour cream, or dried culture. Mix until well incorporated.

3. Cover the container with a plate or lid, and leave it at room temperature for 12 hours.

4. After the culturing time, your cream should have noticeably thickened. Store the crème fraîche in an airtight container in the refrigerator, and use within one to two weeks.

Quark

A relative newcomer to the U.S. culinary landscape, quark has a long history of hearty consumption in Europe. It is typically described as an unaged curd cheese, although the fact that it is made with lactic acid renders it a cultured product. German quark is typically served creamy, containing a good deal of the quark's whey, while other countries prepare theirs with less whey, forming a drier, firmer product. Quark can be made with either cultured buttermilk or yogurt. It is really quite easy to prepare and acts as an incredibly versatile ingredient in a wide variety of dishes.

Quark recipe

Try mixing quark into dips or sauces, especially creamy salad dressings. It also makes a tasty dessert if drizzled with a bit of honey and served alongside fresh fruit; throw in some buttery shortbread cookies if you're feeling especially decadent!

Yield: Slightly more than 4 cups

YOU WILL NEED:

- 4 cups whole, skim, or low-fat milk
- 4 tablespoons cultured buttermilk or yogurt

TO PREPARE:

1. Warm the milk gently in a medium saucepan over medium-high heat until it reaches 105°F (41°C).

2. Transfer the milk to a glass or ceramic container. Using a metal spoon, stir in the buttermilk or yogurt. Mix until well incorporated.

3. Hold the mixture at 105°F (41°C) for the next four hours. Consider any of the "Incubating Ideas" discussed on page 55 for a way to maintain the temperature.

4. After four hours, place the container in the refrigerator. The mixture will thicken slightly during this time. Allow the mixture to cool completely, two to three hours.

5. Once it is chilled, transfer the mixture to a colander lined with butter muslin. Set the colander inside a larger bowl, which will serve as a drip pan. Ladle the curds into the colander, tie the ends of the butter muslin into a knot, and return to the refrigerator. Allow the bag to drain for at least eight hours or overnight.

6. Once drained, transfer the quark from butter muslin to an airtight container, and keep covered in the refrigerator. Use within one to two weeks.

Portrait of a Yogurt Maker

Dave

Dave can take the heat. As owner and head baker at a small production wood-fired bakery, he spends his days in a very hot kitchen. Farm & Sparrow specializes in rustic breads, pastries, and other artisan products. Organic whole grains are stone-milled on site the day of baking. Dough is then mixed by hand and allowed to undergo a long, slow fermentation, allowing natural leavening to occur. The process is finished off with a bake in a wood-fired oven, whose intense heat transforms the dough into a dense, chewy, heady finished product.

During those hot bakes, Dave cools off with homemade yogurt. He sources his milk locally, using the freshest possible. **"I love the taste and richness of fresh raw milk, which in turn makes really good yogurt. Cold raw yogurt sustains me while I'm working long mornings in a very hot bakery."** Once a week, he whips up a fresh batch of yogurt to help him combat his kitchen's heat. Perhaps his yogurt is the secret to his success. Given the incomparable flavor, texture, and aroma of his bakery's products, he's clearly onto something good.

Chapter 6
Cheese

Cheese is quite possibly *the* universal dairy product. Cultures the world over have nuanced it, celebrated it, and given it their own signature twists. Now you can put your spin on this beloved global food, feeling confident in the knowledge that your end product will be free of the additives and preservatives often added to commercially prepared cheeses.

Home cheese-making is an exceptionally good way to get a bit closer to the cheeses you have known and loved for so long. It's also much easier than many people think. Grab a gallon or two of milk, follow my home-kitchen-tested recipes, and you'll be savoring homemade mascarpone, Swiss, and mozzarella in no time. Invite friends or family over for a cheese-centered dinner, and watch their jaws drop in wonder when you tell them you crafted it yourself!

BASIC TECHNIQUES

Cheese-making involves many of the same steps, no matter if you're making paneer or provolone. The constants include milk, heat of some degree, bacteria, and often rennet. The variation comes in temperature, how the curd is handled, types of cultures and milk used, and whether you will be pressing or drying your cheese.

The basic techniques involved in making cheese at home are detailed below. Those steps that are used only in certain types of cheese, such as hard cheeses, will be noted accordingly. When you start making your cheese, refer back to these instructions as needed. They'll provide more detailed explanations of each step than those offered in individual recipes.

1 Heating the Milk

The first step in cheese-making, whether you're making a soft or hard cheese, is heating the milk. The increase in temperature helps to expedite the conversion of lactose to lactic acid. This enables the bacterial cultures added to the milk to grow, helping coagulation (the formation of curds) and helping curds to later separate from whey.

It's very important to closely monitor the temperature of the milk as it heats. If allowed to overheat, the milk's ability to interact properly with the starter culture will be compromised. So, while it's said that a watched pot never boils, a watched pot of milk never overheats! Keep your dairy thermometer handy and check often, stirring frequently to ensure the even distribution of heat.

Milk can be heated in one of two ways: Directly or indirectly. (In the recipes in this book, I will indicate whether direct or indirect heating is to be used.) In direct heating, milk is warmed in a pot set directly over a heat source. Indirect heating warms milk to the desired temperature by means of a double boiler or a sink filled with hot water. If you opt to use a double boiler, remember that the water in the bottom pot shouldn't make contact with the underside of the pot on top. Also, keep water to a gentle simmer, instead of a full, rolling boil. To use the water bath method, put a pot or metal bowl containing the milk in the sink and fill the sink with water warmed to approximately 10 degrees hotter than the target temperature.

2 Adding Starter

Next up in the cheese-making process is the addition of a starter to the warmed milk. Starters include mesophilic and thermophilic cultures in their various forms (see "Starter Cultures" on page 21 for more information). Other recipes call for vinegar or cultured dairy products, such as yogurt, sour cream, or buttermilk. Starters aid in coagulation and begin the acidification process, imparting the flavors characteristic to certain cheeses.

3 Including Additives

For some types of cheeses, additives such as calcium chloride, annatto, lipase, molds, or flavorings may be used. These additives all must be diluted in sterilized water before use. (Using nonsterilized water runs the risk of introducing nasty contaminants such as chlorine that have no place in cheese.) Simply boil the amount of water you'll need, allow it to come to room temperature, and then store it in a clean, sterilized bottle in your refrigerator until needed. When a recipe in this book calls for an additive requiring dilution, it will be noted in the ingredient listing.

4 Adding Rennet

Rennet is used in cheese-making to separate the curds from the whey. It's a fickle muse, however, so take care when adding it to your heated milk. Follow the recipe and measure carefully, or you could end up with a cheese that refuses to set or an acrid, noncompliant curd.

As with additives, rennet will need to be diluted prior to use, regardless of whether your rennet is a liquid, a

powder, or a tablet (see page 23 for more information on available forms of rennet). When called for in a recipe, instructions to dilute rennet will be noted in the ingredient listing. Once diluted, rennet must be evenly dispersed within the milk. This is achieved by stirring the milk constantly for 30 seconds, being certain that your stirring spoon reaches all the way to the bottom of the pot. You'll then cover the pot with a lid, leaving the curd to set.

5 Setting Curds

This is a rest step. Letting your pot sit allows the milk to properly sour. Temperature variations and too much jostling and movement can upset the acidification process, so no dance parties in the kitchen once your curd begins its slumber! Take note of the curdling time indicated in the recipe, and let the pot sit undisturbed the entire time.

6 Cutting Curds

Once your curds have set, it's time to cut them. Cutting the curds releases the whey from the curd, allowing the curd to form a mass that will dry out and solidify into one block during aging. You'll know you've reached the right stage

for cutting when you achieve what's known as a "clean break." This is what is seen when you insert your finger, a knife, or a thermometer into the curd and it breaks away cleanly and clearly. If you test and a clean break doesn't form, wait five or so minutes and then check again.

Once you're sure your curd has set, it's time to start cutting. The manner in which your cheese will be cut is determined by what type of cheese it will ultimately become—soft or hard. Adhere to the following cutting instructions depending on what you are making.

6 A Soft Cheese Curd Cutting

With soft cheeses and bacteria- and mold-ripened cheeses, it's best to not disturb the curd too much. The less interference at this stage, the more velvety your cheese will ultimately be. Using a large perforated ladle, gently scoop out spoonfuls of curd. Transfer the curds to either a cheese mold or a butter muslin-lined colander, as indicated in your recipe.

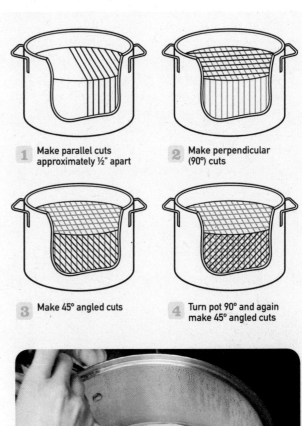

1. Make parallel cuts approximately ½" apart

2. Make perpendicular (90°) cuts

3. Make 45° angled cuts

4. Turn pot 90° and again make 45° angled cuts

6 B Hard Cheese Curd Cutting

To cut the curds effectively, you'll need to be able to cut all the way to the bottom of your pot. This is best achieved by using a knife with a long blade, such as a bread knife or a curd knife, whose sole purpose in life is this very task. To the best of your ability, form straight cuts 1/2 inch apart, slicing at a 90° angle from one side of the pot clear across. Once you've cut across horizontally, turn your pot 90° and begin cutting vertically, in the same consistent-width manner, until you've cut a checkerboard pattern. After you've cut in both directions, turn the pot back to the original direction and begin cutting again, on a 45° angle this time. Turn the pot one last time and cut again along those lines, again on a 45° angle. You have now successfully cut your cheese!

7 Stirring Curds (Hard Cheeses Only)

When making hard cheeses, the curds will need to be stirred just a bit after they are cut, but before they are heated. This allows any residual whey to drain out of the curds. After cutting the curds, allow them to rest for five minutes. Then, using a perforated metal spoon, give the curds a gentle stir. Turn them over each other, being certain to reach all the way to the bottom of the pot. If you see any oversized curds, cut them into ½-inch cubes.

8 Heating Curds (Hard Cheeses Only)

After the curd has been cut and stirred, it will be lightly heated. This forces any remaining whey from the curd, resulting in a firmer curd when it is eventually molded and pressed.

Firmer curds are what you want, as they provide the body needed for the cheese to meld together into one mass during pressing. Heat is introduced to the curds very slowly using a double boiler or a hot water bath, incrementally raising the heat by two degrees every five to 10 minutes. As they warm, the curds will begin to shrink and force out the whey. The curds are held at the temperature indicated in your recipe for the specified period of time and then removed from the heat for draining.

9 Draining

Draining is the next-to-last attempt at removing any sneaky, hold-out whey remaining in the curd. The manner in which your curds will be drained is determined by what type of cheese you are making: hard, soft, or mold- or bacteria-ripened.

9 A Hard Cheese Draining

Transfer the curds to a cheesecloth-lined colander, strainer, or large sieve. Place the colander inside a large bowl to collect the dripping whey. Make sure the colander sits high enough above the bottom of the collecting bowl

to not touch the gathering whey as it rises. Allow the curd to drain for the duration indicated in your recipe.

9 B Soft Cheese Draining

For soft cheeses, the curds are drained just after you cut them, skipping the steps for stirring and heating. Carefully transfer the curds to a butter muslin-lined colander, strainer, or large sieve. Next, tie the four corners of the butter muslin into a strong, secure knot. Suspend the knotted bag either

over the sink, using the faucet to secure it, or thread a wooden spoon through the center of the knot and hang the bag over a pot large enough to collect the dripping whey. I like to wrap a bungee cord around my bag and hang the cord from the sink faucet. Allow the bag to drain for the duration indicated in your recipe.

9C Mold- and Bacteria-ripened Cheese Draining

Transfer the curds directly to cheese molds. Place the filled molds over open racks that are in turn placed over a rectangular collecting container, such as a baking pan or a plastic bin. You can use old refrigerator racks, broiler pan racks, cookie cooling racks, or any other similar rack. Allow the

cheese to drain for the duration indicated in your recipe.

10 Milling Curds (Hard Cheeses Only)

After the curds have drained, gently transfer them to a large glass, metal, or ceramic bowl. Using your fingertips, very delicately break up the curds into smaller pieces. The required size will be indicated by your recipe. Be very gentle here, as rough-handling the curd at this point could cause a potentially disastrous loss of butterfat, a definite no-no. Whatever you do, don't squeeze the curd. You need all the moisture to stay inside where it belongs.

11 Salting

As discussed in the Ingredients chapter, salt serves a number of vital functions in home cheese-making. It helps draw out moisture, puts the kibosh on opportunistic bacteria, and, of course, contributes to flavor. Additionally, it slows down growth of lactic acid, beneficial when you are getting ready to age your cheese. Two methods of salting are used, direct salting and brining. Consult your recipe to determine which method you will be using.

11A Direct Salting

This manner of salting involves adding salt granules directly to the curds. Salt soft cheeses directly by transferring the drained curd to a bowl, adding the amount of salt indicated in the recipe, and stirring with a metal spoon. For hard cheeses, transfer the curds to a bowl, sprinkle the amount of salt indicated over the curds, and then, with clean hands, gently incorporate salt throughout. Mold- and bacteria-ripened cheeses are salted after the curd comes out of its mold. Salt is rubbed over the surface of the cheese just prior to the drying stage.

11B Brining

Only certain types of cheese are salted by brining, usually those with relatively short aging times. A brine is

simply a salt and water solution. The curd is submerged in the solution for a specified length of time. Feta is one of the most widely known brined cheeses, its salty taste giving away its vacation spent at the saltwater spa.

12 Molding and Pressing

Molding and pressing are the final attempts at ridding a cheese of any residual whey. Nearly all cheeses are molded, whether into a hand-shaped log, as with chèvre, or packed into a round mold with a follower on top, as with cheddar, for instance. The mold used is determined both by personal preference and requirements of individual cheeses. According to your recipe, allow your curds to reach 65 to 70°F (18 to 21°C). Next, line your mold with cheesecloth if necessary (some cheeses don't require the use of cheesecloth during molding; individual recipes will indicate when the use of cheesecloth is recommended). Spoon the curds into the mold. If your cheese will not be pressed for long, or not at all, pack the curds in loosely. If your cheese will undergo a long pressing time, pack the curds in tightly and snugly.

For hard cheeses, the mold, filled with curd, is now placed into a cheese press. A follower (a top that fits into the mold and is slightly smaller than its circumference) is

placed atop the mold. Pressure is incrementally applied to the mold for a specified period of time. Be careful when applying pressure. Too much could cause the outer rind of your cheese to split, letting bacteria in. Too little could prevent whey from being squeezed out, resulting in cheese that is too dense. Specific pressures and pressing times will be indicated in individual recipes. Generally speaking, the harder the finished cheese, the longer the pressing time.

13 Misting and Aeration
(Mold- and Bacteria-ripened Cheeses Only)

If you are making a mold- or bacteria-ripened cheese, you will need to inoculate your curd. Depending on the variety of cheese you are making, inoculation will occur either before or after molding and pressing. For blue cheeses, holes are made in the inoculated pressed curd with a sterilized tool (the pointy end of a dairy thermometer works dandy). The mold grows rapidly, spreading into the cheese's interior. For

rind mold-ripened cheeses, such as Camembert and Brie, mold is misted onto the outside of the pressed curd. In either case the curd is then placed in a ripening refrigerator and kept at a certain temperature for a specific duration to allow the mold to develop.

14 Drying (Hard Cheeses Only)

After pressing, most hard cheeses require a bit of room-temperature drying. If it's the dog days of summer and your kitchen lacks air conditioning, room temperature might be too warm. Schedule your cheese-making activities so that the drying can be achieved overnight, when it's cooler, or in the coolest part of your house (anything cooler than about 72°F is fine). Gently remove the pressed curd from the mold, and place it on a cheese board or drying mat (refer to the

Equipment chapter for cheese board and drying mat recommendations). Allow the cheese to rest for several days until it feels dry to the touch. In the event that any mold should form on the surface (as in, mold that you didn't intend to be there!), dip a bit of cheesecloth into some vinegar or saltwater, wring it out, and lightly rub the cheese until the mold is gone.

15 Waxing (Hard Cheeses Only)

Once fully dried, some cheeses are waxed to keep them from drying out or molding during aging. Place the cheese in a refrigerator until completely cool. When it is ready, remove it from the refrigerator and rub the entire surface with white vinegar to deter the growth of mold. Next, turn the fan of a stove hood to high. Melt the wax in a double boiler over medium heat (as mentioned in the Equipment chapter, it is best to dedicate a used or worn-out pot exclusively to this purpose, as removing wax from a pan can be difficult, if not impossible). Cheese wax vapors are rather flammable, so take caution. You know the wax is ready when it's fully melted, but never let it boil.

You can apply wax with a brush or by dipping the cheese fully into the wax. Dip a cheese brush or other natural-bristle brush into the wax and brush it over the cheese, completely covering one side. Let it cool, then turn and repeat on the other side. Once the second side has cooled, repeat the process. To dip, quickly dunk the entire cheese mass directly into the wax, coating one side. Take care, as the wax can get quite slippery. Allow the wax to cool and then repeat on the other side. After the second side has cooled, repeat the process. If any mold appears on the wax during aging, just cut it off. Your cheese is fine, nestled snugly inside.

16 Aging

The final step in the home cheese-making process, aging finishes off your cheese, imparting characteristic flavor, texture, and aroma. Just as with wine, a little maturing time allows the cheese to become nuanced and distinctive. Aging times are highly variable, depending on the cheese you are making. Amounts range from a few days to years.

Controlling temperature and humidity during the aging process is essential. Accordingly, you'll need to ensure an environment conducive to the needs of your cheese. Refer to the discussion of a ripening refrigerator, or "modern-day cheese cave," on page 35 for ideas on achieving the proper climatic conditions needed for cheese-making. If you use  a basement, you'll need to monitor the temperature and humidity levels routinely. This can be done with the aid of a thermometer and a hygrometer (a device that measures humidity). You can find a combined meter at a hardware or home building supply store. Hygrometers are also available at pet stores, where they are sold for monitoring the humidity level of reptile tanks.

If you use a refrigerator, set the temperature to 55°F (13°C) and place a bowl of water in the fridge's bottom. Make sure it is always filled with water; otherwise, your humidity level could become imbalanced.

You will need to turn your cheese periodically as it ages to ensure that the moisture, fat, and proteins in the cheese are distributed evenly and don't end up all smushed together on one side. Turning also prevents the buildup of moisture on the cheese bottom, which could in turn lead to rot. You don't want to have come this far along in the game only to be outdone by a bit of moisture, do you? Turn your cheese as indicated in your recipe, and stop moisture in its tracks.

S oft, unripened, unaged cheeses are the very best place
to begin your cheese-making adventures. They're easy
to make, most are ready to eat within several hours, and all

processing. These cheeses are generally spreadable, creamy,
and milder in both flavor and aroma than aged cheeses,
which develop sharper, more piquant, pungent tastes and

Queso Blanco

Prep Time: 45 to 60 minutes
Draining Time: 3 to 5 hours
Heating Method: Direct

If you're a fan of Central and South American cuisines, chances are you've rubbed shoulders with queso blanco. Mildly sweet, this soft cheese is a perfect partner to spicy foods, providing a creamy, cool counterpoint to the heat of chilies. It is also rather firm, making it perfect for frying or broiling, as it retains its body and shape. Queso blanco is ideal if you want to make your own cheese but find yourself short on time, as it can be made and used the same day. *Yield: Approximately 1 pound*

YOU WILL NEED:

1 gallon whole goat's or cow's milk

¼ teaspoon calcium chloride mixed with ¼ cup cold, sterilized water*

5 tablespoons apple cider vinegar

*Omit if using raw milk.

TO PREPARE:

1. In a medium saucepan, gradually warm the milk to 175 to 180°F (79 to 82°C) directly over medium-low heat. Monitor the temperature closely with a dairy thermometer to avoid overheating. Expect this to take 30 to 35 minutes.

2. Once you reach 175°F (79°C), hold the milk at that temperature for 10 to 12 minutes. Stir the pot frequently to keep the milk from scalding. Add the calcium chloride, if using, and stir for one minute.

3. Add the vinegar a little bit at a time, stirring continuously. Within five to 10 minutes you will see curds begin to form. Continue stirring until all the vinegar has been added and curds are visibly forming.

4. Ladle the curds into a colander, drainer, or large sieve lined with butter muslin or a double layer of cheesecloth. Allow the curds to drain for three to five hours, until you no longer see any whey dripping from the bag.

5. Consume the queso blanco immediately or place it in a lidded container and store in the refrigerator. Use within one week.

Cream Cheese

Prep/Cook Time: 20 to 30 minutes
Ripening/Draining/Aging Time: 36 hours
Heating Method: Indirect

Creamy, light, and couldn't be any easier to make, homemade cream cheese proves that there really is no substitute for handcrafted dairy goods. Cream cheese is infinitely adaptable—try it whipped into pumpkin cheesecake, slathered atop poppy seed bagels, or blended with herbs and veggies and stuffed into mushroom caps. This recipe requires a 24-hour ripening time and a 10-hour draining period, so if you plan to incorporate it into a dish, you'll need to get cracking a couple of days before. *Yield: Approximately 1½ cups*

YOU WILL NEED:

3 cups whole milk

3 cups heavy cream

½ teaspoon (1 packet) direct-set mesophilic starter culture or 2 ounces fresh mesophilic starter culture

¼ teaspoon calcium chloride mixed with ¼ cup cold, sterilized water*

2 drops liquid rennet

*Omit if using raw milk.

TO PREPARE:

1. Combine the milk and cream in the top half of a double boiler or a metal bowl and indirectly warm it to 72°F (22°C), using either a double boiler or a warm water bath.

2. Add the starter culture to the milk, and stir the mixture with a metal spoon to fully incorporate. Add the calcium chloride, if using, and stir for one minute. Add the rennet and stir again to combine. Remove the pot from the heat source, cover with a lid, and place in a draft-free spot at room temperature. Allow it to sit for 24 hours.

3. The next day, the curds should look like very firm pieces of yogurt. Transfer the curds and whey into a colander, drainer, or large sieve lined with butter muslin or a double layer of cheesecloth. Tie the four corners of the butter muslin or cheesecloth into a knot. Either hang the bag over a sink to drain, or place a wooden spoon or chopstick through the knot and suspend the bag over a catch bowl. Allow the curds to drain for 10 hours at room temperature.

4. Once you no longer see any whey dripping from the bag, remove the curds from the cheesecloth and transfer them to a small, lidded bowl. Give the curds a good stir until they look spreadable and creamy.

5. Cover your cream cheese and place it in the refrigerator for at least one hour. You can use it immediately or store it in the refrigerator and use within one to two weeks.

Mascarpone

Cook Time: 20 to 25 minutes
Aging Time: 12 hours
Heating Method: Direct

This soft cheese lends itself to a wide variety of uses beyond tiramisu, the Italian dessert combining mascarpone with espresso and ladyfingers. The flavor and texture of mascarpone can be found at the intersection of a mildly tangy sour cream, whipped cream, and cream cheese. Spread it on quick breads (pumpkin in winter, zucchini in summer) or try it in a tart (caramelized apple in autumn, rhubarb and strawberries in spring)—there's no end to the opportunities presented by this subtly sweet-and-sour cheese. It needs half of a day to set up, though, so if you intend to serve it with dinner, you'll need to get started early. *Yield: Approximately 1 pound*

YOU WILL NEED:

4 cups half-and-half or light cream*

¼ teaspoon (1 packet) direct-set crème fraîche starter culture

*You can also make your own half-and-half by combining 1 cup heavy whipping cream with 3 cups whole milk. Whisk the milk and cream together to fully incorporate before use.

TO PREPARE:

1. In a medium saucepan, gradually warm the half-and-half to 86°F (30°C) directly over low heat. Monitor the temperature closely with a dairy thermometer to avoid overheating.

2. Stir in the starter culture with a metal spoon, and then remove the pan from the heat. Cover, and allow the mixture to rest at room temperature for 12 hours. When your curds have set, they will look like a very thick yogurt or cream.

3. At this point, depending on your desired thickness and consistency, the mascarpone is done. If you'd like it to be a bit firmer (as is necessary for dishes such as tiramisu), ladle the curds into a colander, drainer, or large sieve lined with butter muslin or a double layer of cheesecloth. Put a catch bowl underneath the colander, place in the refrigerator, and allow the cheese to drain for two to three hours.

4. Use the mascarpone immediately, or place it in a lidded container and store in the refrigerator. Use within two to three weeks.

Feta

Prep Time: 3 hours
Draining Time: 4 to 5 hours
Heating Method: Indirect

Feta is one of my personal must-haves when it comes to cheese. It is almost always found in the cheese drawer of my refrigerator, ready to adorn the humblest of salads, be tucked into fish tacos, or be crumbled atop a homemade pizza. Traditionally made from both sheep's and goat's milk, this salty cheese has been a Mediterranean culinary staple for centuries. In this recipe I use goat's milk alone; unless you keep sheep or have a neighbor who does; collecting the required quantity of sheep's milk can prove challenging. *Yield: Approximately 1½ pounds*

YOU WILL NEED:

1	gallon goat's milk
½	teaspoon (1 packet) direct-set mesophilic starter culture or 2 ounces fresh starter culture
¼	teaspoon calcium chloride mixed with ¼ cup cold, sterilized water*
1	teaspoon liquid rennet (or ½ tablet, crushed)
¼	cup cold, sterilized water
2 to 3	tablespoons cheese salt or kosher salt, to taste

*Omit if using raw milk.

TO PREPARE:

1. Warm the milk to 88°F (31°C) indirectly, using either a double boiler or a water bath in the sink (see page 65 for water bath instructions).

2. Add the starter culture, and stir with a metal spoon to fully incorporate. Remove the mixture from the heat source, cover, wrap with a kitchen towel, and allow to sit for one hour.

3. Add the calcium chloride, if using, and stir for one minute to combine. In a small bowl, mix the rennet into the water. Stir to thoroughly combine, then whisk the rennet into the milk, making certain that it is distributed evenly. Cover the pot again, and allow it to sit for an additional hour. The curd is ready when a clean break forms (see page 66).

4. Cut the curds into 1-inch cubes. Allow the curds to rest for 15 minutes, then gently stir the curds for 20 minutes using a metal spoon. This allows the curds and whey to separate more fully from one another, resulting in a firmer feta.

5. Transfer the curds and whey into a colander, drainer, or large sieve lined with butter muslin or a double layer of cheesecloth. Tie the four corners of the butter muslin or cheesecloth into a knot. Either hang the bag over a sink to drain, or place a wooden spoon or chopsticks through the knot and suspend the bag over a catch bowl. Allow the curds to drain for four to five hours.

6. Unwrap the bag, place the ball of curd on a cutting board, and cut the curd into 1¹/₂-inch slices. Cut the slices into approximately 1-inch cubes.

7. Place the cubes into a lidded container, sprinkle with salt to taste, cover, and place in refrigerator. I like a salty feta, so I tend to opt for the upper amount of suggested salt. If you prefer an even stronger, extra-salty feta, prepare a brine by mixing 8 cups warm water with 1 cup cheese salt. Stir until the salt is completely dissolved in the water. Add unsalted 1-inch feta cubes to the brine, cover with a lid, and store in the refrigerator.

8. Allow the feta to cure for four days and then use within three weeks. If brined, use within one month.

Paneer

Prep Time: 25 minutes
Draining Time: 3 hours
Heating Method: Direct

Saag paneer is one of my all-time favorite Indian dishes, made from a savory blend of cream, spinach, spices, and cubes of this soft cheese. We often make it at home, especially during the spring when my garden is exploding with fresh spinach. Served alongside a bit of tandoori spice-rubbed salmon or catfish and a piece of ghee- and chutney-laden naan, it's quite possibly the perfect meal. Paneer is also delicious in any type of curry, or simply cubed up and pan-fried in a bit of ghee or butter. *Yield: Approximately 1 pound*

YOU WILL NEED:

8 cups whole milk

¼ teaspoon calcium chloride mixed with ¼ cup cold, sterilized water*

4 ½ tablespoons lemon juice

*Omit if using raw milk.

TO PREPARE:

1. In a medium saucepan, heat the milk to a gentle boil. Stir the pot every few minutes to keep the milk from scorching. Add the calcium chloride, if using, and stir for one minute to combine.

2. Reduce the heat to low and stir in the lemon juice. The milk should begin to coagulate. If that fails to occur, add an additional 1 tablespoon lemon juice and watch for the whey to become clear, as opposed to milky. Once curds begin to form, remove the pot from the heat, cover, and allow to rest for five minutes.

3. Ladle the curds into a colander, drainer, or large sieve lined with butter muslin or a double layer of cheesecloth. Place a catch bowl underneath to collect the whey as it drains off.

4. Tie the four corners of the butter muslin or cheesecloth into a knot. Give the knot a light squeeze to remove the whey. Place the knotted bag onto a rimmed cookie sheet. On top of the bag, put a heavy board, such as a wooden or thick plastic cutting board. Place a weight on top of the board. You could use a stack of heavy books, a gallon-sized jar filled with water, or a brick or two. You're simply trying to weigh down the curd to force any whey out. Leave the curds to drain and firm for three hours.

5. Remove the paneer from the cheesecloth, and transfer it to a lidded container. Use it immediately or store in the refrigerator and use within one week.

Ricotta

Prep/Cook Time: 1 hour
Draining Time: 20 to 50 minutes
Heating Method: Direct

Soft, creamy, easy ricotta—is there anything better? Minimum processing produces maximum satisfaction with this delicious cheese. Traditionally, ricotta is made with cow, sheep, or goat whey left over from making other cheeses. However, I've found it difficult to make whey-based ricotta, as the gathered whey must be used within an hour or so after collection. Unless you make cheese every day, chances are you won't have just-made whey on hand when you want to make ricotta. This recipe solves that problem: you can make an equally tasty ricotta using milk. It is creamier than whey-based ricotta, which I happen to think is a good thing. If you want your ricotta to be drier, simply allow it to drain for an additional 20 to 30 minutes. Fresh ricotta is delectable layered in an herbaceous lasagna, baked into a ricotta cheesecake, dolloped onto pizza, or even stirred into pancakes.
Yield: Approximately 1 pound

YOU WILL NEED:

8	cups whole milk
1	cup heavy cream
1/2	cup lemon juice
1/4	teaspoon calcium chloride mixed with 1/4 cup cold, sterilized water*
1/2	teaspoon cheese salt or kosher salt

*Needed only if using homogenized, store-bought milk

TO PREPARE:

1. In a medium saucepan, stir together the milk, cream, and lemon juice with a metal spoon. Gradually warm the mixture to 170°F (77°C) directly over medium-low heat. Monitor the temperature closely with a dairy thermometer to avoid overheating. Expect this to take about 30 minutes. Stir only once or twice while heating to prevent sticking; any more and you run the risk of making the curd too small. Add the calcium chloride, if using, and stir for one minute to combine.

2. Increase the heat gradually until the mixture reaches 200°F (93°C). This will take anywhere from four to seven minutes. Be sure to stop just before the boiling point. Your curds should resemble a creamy, custardy mass at this point.

3. Remove the pot from the heat, and allow to rest for 20 minutes. Meanwhile, line a colander, drainer, or large sieve with butter muslin or a double layer of cheesecloth.

4. Ladle the curds into the colander, and allow them to drain for at least 20 minutes. For a firmer curd, allow the curds to drain an additional 20 to 30 minutes.

5. Transfer the curds to a medium bowl. Add the salt, and stir with a metal spoon to fully incorporate.

6. Use the ricotta immediately, or place it in a lidded container and store in the refrigerator. Use within one week.

Cottage Cheese

Prep/Cook Time: 6 to 8 hours
Draining Time: 20 minutes
Heating Method: Direct

Cottage cheese, also commonly known in some parts of the world as pot cheese, or farmer's cheese, is an incredibly versatile addition to your home dairy repertoire. It's scrumptious on its own as a light snack, but also works well with a variety of ingredients and flavorings. My personal favorite way of enjoying cottage cheese is grinding some fresh black pepper over it and then serving with fresh melon or tossing in a handful of sweet grape tomatoes. Delicious! Cottage cheese is also a fine stand-in for ricotta in lasagna or manicotti, takes well to fresh herbs for a veggie dip, is delectable made into pancakes, and is a welcome addition to quiches and omelets.

Yield: Approximately 1 pound

YOU WILL NEED:

- 1 gallon whole, low-fat, or skim milk
- ¼ teaspoon calcium chloride mixed with ¼ cup cold, sterilized water*
- ½ teaspoon (1 packet) direct-set mesophilic starter culture or 4 ounces fresh starter culture
- 1 tablespoon rennet solution (made from ¼ teaspoon liquid rennet dissolved in ¼ cup sterilized water)
- ¼ cup heavy cream
- 1 teaspoon cheese salt or kosher salt, optional

*Omit if using raw milk.

TO PREPARE:

1. In medium saucepan, warm milk gently over medium heat to 72°F (22°C). Monitor the temperature closely with a dairy thermometer to avoid overheating.

2. Add the starter culture to the milk, stirring with a metal spoon to incorporate thoroughly. Add calcium chloride, if using, and stir for one minute to incorporate. Gently stir in the diluted rennet.

3. Remove the milk from the heat, cover, and allow to sit at room temperature (between 68 and 72°F [20 and 22°C]) for four to six hours, until the curd coagulates.

4. Once the curds have firmed to the clean break stage, cut them into ½-inch cubes (see page 67). Let the cubes rest for 20 minutes.

5. Place the pot of cubed curds over medium heat and very, very gradually, warm to 110°F (43°C). Raise the temperature only about two to four degrees every five minutes. After each five-minute interval, stir the curds gently with a metal spoon. This will take about 35 minutes, or thereabouts.

6. Once you've reached 110°F (43°C), hold the temperature there for the next 25 minutes. The curds will begin to visibly firm up and lose their jellylike texture. To test for doneness, squeeze a curd. If it doesn't feel solid, and instead feels a bit mushy, continue cooking a bit longer and then test again.

7. When you are sure your curds are properly cooked, allow them to rest in the pot for 10 minutes.

8. Next, transfer the curds into a colander, drainer or large sieve lined with butter muslin or a double layer of cheesecloth. Set the colander over a large bowl to catch the whey. Let the curds drain for 10 minutes.

9. Tie the corners of your cheesecloth into a knot. Run the knotted bag under ice cold water for two minutes, or dip the knotted bag into a bowl of ice cold water two or three times. Give the bag a firm squeeze, and place it back into the colander to drain for an additional 10 minutes.

10. Remove the curds from the cheesecloth, and transfer them to a medium bowl. Use your hands to break up any large pieces of curd that may have stuck together.  Add heavy cream and salt, if using, and stir with a metal spoon to incorporate.

11. Either consume immediately or place your finished cottage cheese in a lidded container and store in the refrigerator. Use within one week.

Chèvre

Prep/Cook Time: 12 to 14 hours
Draining Time: 6 to 8 hours
Heating Method: Indirect

French for goat, chèvre is quite possibly one of humankind's oldest cheese varieties; variations of it are consumed all over the world. Customarily, it is made by simply allowing goat's milk to ripen and curdle over the course of several days. Goats are hearty, intrepid creatures, willing to travel to and eat what the more delicate cow can't or won't. Accordingly, the thistles, bitter herbs, or any other manner of vegetation goats consume account for the tangy flavor present in their milk. Chèvre is quite easy to make and can be enjoyed in relatively little time. Served up sweet with fig jam or savory, rolled in fresh herbs or spices, chèvre is a highly versatile, always delicious cheese. *Yield: Approximately 1 pound*

YOU WILL NEED:

1 gallon goat's milk

¼ teaspoon (1 packet) direct-set chèvre starter culture*

¼ teaspoon calcium chloride mixed with ¼ cup cold, sterilized water**

*If you don't have any specifically chèvre starter culture on hand, substitute ¼ teaspoon direct-set mesophilic culture, as well as 1 tablespoon rennet solution made from 1 drop liquid rennet dissolved in 5 tablespoons cold water.

**Omit if using raw milk.

TO PREPARE:

1. Warm the milk to 72°F (22°C) indirectly, using either a double boiler or a warm water bath (see page 65). Monitor the temperature of both the milk and the water bath using a dairy thermometer.

2. Add the starter culture and stir with a metal spoon to fully incorporate. If using a general mesophilic starter culture, whisk in the rennet, making certain that it is evenly distributed. Add the calcium chloride, if using, and stir for one minute to incorporate. Remove the pot from the heat source, cover, wrap with a kitchen towel, and allow the mixture to sit at room temperature (between 68 and 72°F [20 and 22°C]) for 12 hours.

3. The curd is ready when a clean break forms (use your finger or a long-handed knife to check). If, after 12 hours, a clean break isn't visible, allow the curds to sit for several more hours, and then check again. The consistency should resemble a thick yogurt, full of body, but not too firm.

4. Ladle the mixture into a colander, drainer, or large sieve lined with butter muslin or a double layer of cheesecloth. Tie the four corners of the cheesecloth into a knot. Either hang the bag over a sink to drain, or place a wooden spoon or chopsticks through the knot and suspend the bag over a catch bowl. Allow the curds to drain for six to eight hours, or until no whey is visibly dripping from the bag. Alternatively, gently ladle the curds into cheese molds (it is not necessary to line the molds with cheesecloth). Place molds on a rack, such as a cookie cooling rack, placed over a collecting pan, such as a cookie sheet or baking pan. Allow to drain for six to eight hours.

5. After draining, remove the chèvre from the cheesecloth or mold. Consume immediately, or place it in a lidded container and store in the refrigerator. Use within one week.

LOVELY AND DELICIOUS

Nuts and Fruits: walnuts, pecans, pistachios, almonds, tamari almonds, pine nuts, pumpkin seeds, dried cranberries, dried blueberries, crystallized ginger, currants, candied citrus peel, dried apple, dried pear, dried apricot, goji berries

Flowers (petals only): nasturtiums, violets, lavender buds, roses, jasmine, chamomile, bee balm, borage, calendula, hibiscus, Johnny-jump-up, lilac, pansy, sunflower, red clover, scented geranium, marigold, dianthus, elderberry, honeysuckle, linden, tuberous begonia

Condiments: honey, olive tapenade, bee pollen, jam, marmalade, fruit butter, pickled vegetables, sea salt, truffle oil, aged balsamic vinegar (just a drizzle!)

If you'd like to impart a bit of flair to your cheeses for gift giving or a special occasion, there are a number of options for playing "dress up." Consider rolling your cheese in chopped fresh or dried herbs and crushed or ground spices. You could also festoon them with chopped dried fruits and finely chopped toasted nuts. Edible flowers are an unexpected adornment, enhancing both flavor and fragrance, while condiments such as honey, pickled vegetables, or balsamic vinegar are ideal for serving alongside your homemade cheeses. Here are a number of ideas for making your cheeses both delicious and dazzling!

Herbs: basil, chives, parsley, tarragon, mint, rosemary, cilantro, thyme, marjoram, oregano, savory, chervil, dill, herbes de Provence, sage, anise hyssop, lemon balm, fennel fronds

Spices: cumin, black pepper, juniper berries, red pepper flakes, curry powder, fennel seed, celery seed, caraway seed, coriander

Once you've decked out your cheese and swaddled it in flavor and beauty, you'll need to place it on a serving dish. I love using a chalkboard or a chalkboard-painted cutting board and writing the name of each cheese underneath it. A piece of slate would work just as well. A beautiful bamboo cutting board is also a lovely forum for showing your cheeses, as are handcrafted hardwood cheeseboards. Wrapping cheese in grape leaves is another way of adding some pizzazz to your cheese plate. It's also a fine way to prepare cheeses for gifting, as is using parchment or waxed paper, finished off with a bit of twine, raffia, or ribbon.

Mozzarella

A favorite cheese for many, mozzarella has a long-standing reputation of winning hearts and taste buds. Making this soft, stretchy cheese at home is quite simple, permitted you have the correct type of milk. Store-bought milk that has been ultra-pasteurized at high temperatures is completely unusable for mozzarella-making. Such milk will render your curds more like ricotta than the pliant, malleable mass of curd needed for mozzarella stretching. I speak from experience on this topic after wasting 2 gallons of organic milk before figuring out that the milk was actually the culprit. If you cannot access fresh-from-the-cow milk, look for low-pasteurized milk at your grocer or ask them to begin carrying it. **Yield: *Approximately 1 pound***

YOU WILL NEED:

- 1 gallon whole cow's milk (be certain that your milk has not been ultra pasteurized)
- 2 teaspoons citric acid powder
- ¼ teaspoon calcium chloride mixed with ¼ cup cold, sterilized water*
- ½ teaspoon liquid rennet or ¼ crushed tablet
- ¼ cup cold, sterilized water
- 1 teaspoon cheese salt or kosher salt

    *Omit if using raw milk.

TO PREPARE:

1. Place the milk in a large stockpot. Gently stir in the citric acid powder and the calcium chloride. Warm the milk gently, directly over medium heat, to 88°F (31°C). Monitor the temperature closely with a dairy thermometer to avoid overheating.

2. In a small bowl, whisk together the rennet and the cold water. Add the rennet solution to the milk mixture. Continue stirring until the temperature reaches 104 to 106°F (40 to 41°C). Remove the pot from the heat, cover, and allow to rest for 15 to 20 minutes. The curds and whey will begin to separate during this time.

3. Using a slotted metal spoon, remove the curds and place them in a large microwavable glass or ceramic bowl. Press against the mass of curds with the slotted spoon, forcing out as much whey as possible, and pour it off into the pot of whey.

4. You can warm your curds one of two ways: with the microwave or with heated whey.

Microwave: Place the bowl of curds in the microwave and heat on "HIGH" for one minute. Remove the bowl from the microwave and press the curds, using either the slotted spoon or your hand (wear rubber gloves!), forcing out and pouring off any whey. The curds should begin to appear melted. If not, heat for an additional 20 seconds.

Add the salt, and begin kneading the curd mass with either your hands or a metal spoon, folding it over itself repeatedly. It will begin to become shiny and pliant, like taffy. Microwave again on "HIGH" for one minute. Press out any remaining whey. Knead the curd again, until it is quite elastic and begins to stretch out like a piece of chewing gum. If your curd breaks instead of stretching, put it back into the microwave for an additional 30 seconds, and then stretch.

Heated whey: Once you have separated the curds from the whey, warm the pot of whey to 170 to 175°F (77 to 79°C), just before it really gets boiling. Place about one-quarter of the curds into a medium bowl. Sprinkle some of the salt over the curds. Ladle a good amount of the hot whey over the curd mass. Wearing rubber gloves, begin to knead the curd until it begins to melt and stick together. You may need to add more hot whey to the curds to maintain the temperature. Repeat with the next quarter of curd, repeating the above steps until all of the curd has been warmed and stretched in hot whey.

5. Once ready, it will be pliant and spongy and shiny. You can consume the mozzarella immediately, or place it in a lidded container and store in the refrigerator. Use within one to two weeks.

"Bend Me, Shape Me, Anyway You Want Me": DIY Cheese Molds

Containers intended for other purposes can be cheaply and easily transformed into cheese-molding vessels.

YOGURT CONTAINERS

Commercially prepared plastic yogurt containers work quite well as inexpensive soft cheese molds. Simply clean out the container thoroughly, and then, using a hammer and nail or a drill, puncture the bottom and sides of the container with multiple small holes.

PLASTIC STORAGE CONTAINERS

Any home supply or grocery store will offer plastic storage containers for purchase. Opt for multiples of the same size, or choose a variety of sizes appropriately proportioned for containing a small amount of cheese. Puncture the sides and bottom as described at left, and you're all set to be the big cheese (maker, that is).

Stayin' Alive

After putting the effort into making homemade cheeses, you'll want to do all you can to preserve their shelf life. Temperature and humidity, location, and storage container all come into play when considering how to best store cheeses. The shelf life of cheeses is highly variable, with soft and fresh cheeses lasting considerably less time (one to two weeks) than their harder cousins, which can last for months.

TEMPERATURE & HUMIDITY

Cheese requires a precise range of temperature and humidity levels in order to keep well. Ideally, cheese should be stored between 35 and 45°F (2 and 7°C). Humidity levels should range between 65 and 75 percent.

LOCATION

In order to keep your cheese at the necessary temperature and humidity, store it in a warmer area of your refrigerator, such as a bottom vegetable crisper drawer. Don't use any storage bins on the door, as temperature fluctuations can cause cheese to deteriorate.

CONTAINERS & WRAPPING

Wrap hard cheese loosely in cheesecloth, parchment paper, or wax paper, and place in the crisper drawer. Allow your cheese to breathe or it will dry out. Change the wrapping every three to four days. Store soft cheeses like feta and Brie in glass or plastic lidded containers. I store both homemade and purchased cheeses unwrapped in rectangular glass storage containers with plastic lids. Folded paper towels on the bottom of the container, changed out weekly, collect moisture. Aside from strong-smelling cheeses like Gorgonzola that require individual storage containers, it's perfectly fine to place different cheeses beside one another in this method.

HELPFUL TIPS

→ If your cheese seems especially dry, smells "off," or develops slime or sludge, consider it a loss and throw it out.

→ If your cheese develops mold, simply cut it off about 1/2 inch down into the cheese block. This ensures you've removed invisible mold fibers that reach down further.

→ Soft, fresh cheeses that are stored in a brine or in whey don't need to have their solution changed out. These cheeses are intended to be consumed within a short enough time span that the preserving liquid should remain fresh.

→ It's not advisable to freeze those cheeses that you intend to serve fresh. Freezing alters a cheese's texture and flavor. If you do elect to freeze a cheese, its best use is for cooking. Some hard cheeses should be grated before freezing, as attempting to do so afterwards is a task of Sisyphean proportions. Don't freeze cheese any longer than two months, and be sure to thaw it out in the refrigerator rather than at room temperature.

Advanced Cheeses

Hard and mold- or bacteria-ripened cheeses are considerably more involved than their soft cousins. They require a greater amount of processing, will need to spend time in a cheese press, and must have very specific climatic conditions met in order to ripen properly. That said, for the inspired cheese-maker, they are the next logical step after dabbling in fresh and unaged cheeses.

The following recipes present an offering of hard, Italian, and mold- and bacteria-ripened cheeses. A number of exceptionally well-written, advanced, artisan home cheese-making books are available for those desiring to make an even greater variety of cheeses.

Cheddar

Cheddar

Prep/Cook Time: 6 ½ hours
Draining Time: 20 minutes
Pressing Time: 36 hours
Aging Time: minimum of 3 months
Heating Method: Indirect

One of the most popular cheeses in both the United States and the United Kingdom, the term *cheddar* is both a noun, referring to the cheese itself, and a verb. To cheddar a cheese means to cut the curd into cubes, salt it, and then stack and repeatedly turn it prior to pressing. The intensity of a particular cheddar's flavor is reflective of its vintage, or aging period. In the following recipe, I've offered a cheddar made in the traditional manner, utilizing the cheddaring technique. It takes longer to age than a farmhouse-style cheddar (which omits the cheddaring process and is usually ready in four weeks), but produces an end product that is creamy and delicious. Try cheddar scattered over a tomato and marjoram frittata, melted over warm apple pie, or unadorned alongside fresh fruits, whole-wheat crackers, and a spicy chutney (my personal favorite). *Yield: Approximately 2 pounds*

YOU WILL NEED:

- 2 gallons whole milk
- ½ teaspoon (1 packet) direct-set mesophilic starter culture or 4 ounces fresh starter culture
- ¼ teaspoon calcium chloride mixed with ¼ cup cold, sterilized water*
- 1 teaspoon liquid rennet (or ½ tablet, crushed)
- ¼ cup cold, sterilized water
- Cheese salt or kosher salt
- Cheese wax

*Omit if using raw milk

TO PREPARE:

1. Warm the milk to 86°F (30°C) indirectly by use of either a double boiler or a water bath in the sink (see page 65). Monitor the temperature of both the milk and the water bath using a dairy thermometer. Add the starter culture, and stir with a metal spoon to fully incorporate. Cover, and hold at 86°F (30°C) for one hour.

2. Add the calcium chloride, if using, and stir for one minute. In a small bowl, whisk together the rennet and cold water. Slowly add the rennet solution to the milk mixture, and stir gently for one minute to fully incorporate. Cover again, and allow the mixture to sit at 86°F (30°C) for an additional hour.

3. Check for a clean break. If curds cling to your cutting knife, allow the curds to sit and ripen for a bit longer. Once a clean break is achieved, cut the curds into ½-inch cubes. Allow the cut curd to sit for 10 minutes.

4. Slowly heat the curd to 100°F (38°C). Do this very gradually, increasing the temperature only one degree every one to three minutes. Stir frequently with a ladle, and gently cut any large pieces of curd that you may find.

5. Once you've reached 100°F (38°C), hold the temperature there for 30 minutes. Stir the curd frequently. The curds should begin to shrink and reduce significantly in size. Remove the pot from the heat source, and allow the curds to rest for 20 minutes.

6. Ladle the curds out of the pot and into a colander, drainer, or large sieve lined with a double layer of cheesecloth. Allow to drain for 20 minutes.

7. Remove the curds from the drainer and place onto a large cutting board. The curds should stick together, as one big mass. Cut the curds into slices around 3 inches long and ½ inch thick. This process is the beginning of cheddaring.

8. Fill your kitchen sink with water approximately 100 to 105°F (38 to 41°C). Place the curd slices into the pot used for warming, put the pot into the sink, and cover it with a lid. Maintain the temperature for two hours, turning the curd slices every 20 minutes or so. After two hours, the curds should feel rubbery and springy, and bounce back when pushed with your finger.

9. Take the pot out of the water and use a long-handled knife to cut the curd into smaller cubes, between ½ and ¾ inch square. Return the pot to the sink basin of warm water. Maintain the temperature for an additional 30 to 35 minutes. Use your fingers or a slotted metal spoon, and turn the curds gently about every seven to eight minutes to keep them from matting.

10. After 30 to 35 minutes, remove the pot from the sink basin. Sprinkle 2 tablespoons cheese salt over the curds, and stir in gently with a slotted spoon.

11. Ladle the curds out of the pot and into a 2-pound cheese mold lined with cheesecloth. If you are using a mold with an open bottom, place whatever you will be using as your drip pan underneath the cheese mold while you do this to provide a solid base for the mold (otherwise, once you transfer the mold to the cheese press, your curd will spill out everywhere).

12. Once the curds are all ladled into the cheese mold, fold the excess cheesecloth over the top, place the follower in, and press the curd at 15 pounds of pressure for 10 minutes.

13. Take the cheese mold out of the press, remove the curd from the mold, and unwrap the cheesecloth. Change out the cheesecloth with a fresh, clean dressing, return the curd to the cheese mold, place the mold back into the cheese press, and press again at 40 pounds of pressure for 12 hours.

14. Repeat the process again, re-dressing the curd, and press at 50 pounds of pressure for 12 hours. Repeat the process one final time, re-dressing the curd, and press at 50 pounds of pressure for an additional 12 hours, for a total pressing time of 36 hours.

15. Next, remove the curd from the mold, and unwrap the cheesecloth. Place it on a cheeseboard or cheese mat, and air-dry for three to four days. Turn the cheese daily, and keep it dry.

16. After three days, you'll need to wax your cheese. Refer to page 71 for detailed instructions.

17. Store your cheese at 50 to 55°F (10 to 13°C) for at least three months, longer for a sharper flavor. Try to remember to turn it daily.

18. If you own a cheese trier (refer to page 33 for a detailed description of this nifty cheese-testing tool), you can test the cheese at three months to see if the flavor is to your liking. Otherwise, wait a bit longer before consuming your cheddar, as the flavors improve with aging. Once ready, store in the refrigerator and use within one month.

Swiss

Prep/Cook Time: 3 hours
Pressing Time: 15 to 16 hours
Brining Time: 12 hours
Aging Time: 3 months
Heating Method: Indirect

Long thought by young children to be the vestige of marauding mice, the holes in Swiss cheese are actually the result of bacteria—*Propionic shermanii*. This bacteria is responsible for both the flavor and physical appearance of Swiss-style cheeses. Carbon dioxide given off by the bacteria causes the cheese to swell during aging, forcing the characteristic holes into the curd. Specific types of Swiss cheese are named for the areas in Switzerland from which they hail, including Emmenthal and Gruyere. From the robustness of a Reuben to the comfort of a warm fondue, try your hand at this "holiest" of cheeses. **Yield: Approximately 2 pounds**

YOU WILL NEED:

- 2 gallons whole milk
- 1/2 teaspoon (1 packet) direct-set thermophilic starter culture or 4 ounces fresh starter culture
- 1 teaspoon powdered *Propionic shermanii*
- 1/4 teaspoon calcium chloride mixed with 1/4 cup cold, sterilized water*
- 1/2 teaspoon liquid rennet (or 1/4 tablet, crushed)
- 1/4 cup cold, sterilized water
- 4 cups cheese salt or kosher salt

  *Omit if using raw milk.

TO PREPARE:

1. Warm the milk to 90°F (32°C) indirectly, using either a double boiler or a warm water bath (see page 65). Monitor the temperature of both the milk and the water bath using a dairy thermometer.

2. Add the starter culture to the milk, and stir with a metal spoon to fully incorporate. Scoop out 1/4 cup of the milk, and mix with the *Propionic shermanii*. Add the mixture back to the pot, stirring well to evenly disperse the bacteria. Cover the pot and hold at 90°F (32°C) for 15 minutes.

3. Add in calcium chloride, if using, and stir for one minute. In a small bowl, whisk together the rennet and 1/4 cup cold water. Slowly add the rennet solution to the milk mixture, and stir gently to fully incorporate. Cover the pot again and allow it to sit, maintaining 90°F (32°C), for 30 minutes.

4. Check for a clean break. If curds cling to the cutting knife, allow the curds to sit and ripen for a bit longer. Once a clean break is achieved, cut the curds into 1/4-inch cubes.

5. After the curd has been cut, slowly stir it with a ladle for the next 45 minutes. This forces whey out of the curds gradually, before the curds are heated further. Hold the temperature at 90°F (32°C) for the entire duration. As you stir, the curd will become smaller and smaller as whey is forced from the curd. This is what you want. If you see any large chunks of curd, use the ladle to cut them into smaller pieces. This process is known as *foreworking*, which simply means to gradually warm the curd up before cooking it.

6. Slowly heat the curd to 120°F (49°C). Do this very gradually, increasing the temperature only one degree every one to three minutes. Once you've reached 120°F (49°C), hold the temperature there for the next 25 minutes. Test to see if your curds are ready to be pressed by removing a couple of tablespoons and squeezing them together in the palm

of your hand. If they break apart into individual pieces, you're all set. If they hold fast to each other, continue to cook a few minutes longer and then test for doneness again.

7. Ladle the hot curds out of the pot and into a 2-pound cheese mold lined with cheesecloth. Do this carefully, yet quickly, as it is essential that the curds be hot for pressing. If you are using a mold with an open bottom, place whatever you will be using as your drip pan underneath the cheese mold while you do this, so as to provide a solid base for the mold (otherwise, once you transfer the mold to the cheese press, your curd will spill out everywhere).

8. Once the curds are all ladled into the cheese mold, fold the excess cheesecloth over the top, place the follower in, and press the curd at 10 pounds of pressure for 30 minutes.

9. Take the cheese mold out of the press, remove the curd from the mold, and unwrap the cheesecloth. Change out the cheesecloth with a fresh, clean dressing, return the curd to the cheese mold, place the mold back into the cheese press, and press at 10 pounds of pressure for an additional 30 minutes.

10. Repeat the process again, re-dressing the curd, and press at 15 pounds of pressure for two hours. Repeat one final time, re-dressing the curd, and press at 15 pounds of pressure for 12 to 14 hours.

11. Prepare a brine by dissolving the salt in 1 gallon cold water. Use a stainless-steel, glass, plastic, or ceramic container, as aluminum could corrode. Dip a bit of cheesecloth into the brine, wring it out over the sink, and set it aside to dry out. Next, remove the curd from the mold, unwrap the cheesecloth, and submerge it in the brine. Place the container in the refrigerator, and allow the curd to soak in the brine for 12 hours.

12. Remove the curd from the brine, pat dry with the dry, salted cheesecloth, and place the cheese on a cheeseboard or cheese mat. Store it in either a basement or a ripening refrigerator (see "Ripening Refrigerator" on page 35 for a discussion of home-ripening) at 50 to 55°F (10 to 13°C) and 85 percent humidity for one week. Adjust the humidity, if necessary, by placing a bowl of warm water next to the cheese. Turn the cheese daily, and wipe it with a dry, salted cheesecloth.

13. After one week, transfer the cheese to a warm room with high humidity, such as a kitchen or pantry, and a temperature between 68 and 74°F (20 and 23°C). Keep it there for two to three weeks, turning it every day and continuing to wipe it with a dry, salted cheesecloth. The cheese will begin to swell during this period, as carbon dioxide is given off by the *Propionic shermanii*, causing holes to form inside the cheese.

14. Once the holes, or "eyes," are visible, transfer the cheese one last time back to your basement or ripening refrigerator. Keep at 45 to 50°F (7 to 10°C) and 85 percent humidity for three to six months. Monitor the humidity regularly, adding a bowl of warm water beside the cheese if needed. Turn and wipe the cheese with a dry, salted cheesecloth every few days.

15. Wait a minimum of three months before consuming your Swiss cheese. If you own a cheese trier, you can test the cheese at three months to see if the flavor is to your liking. Once ready, store in the refrigerator and use within three weeks.

Parmesan

Prep/Cook Time: 2 hours
Pressing Time: 15 to 17 hours
Brining Time: 24 hours
Aging Time: 6 to 10 months
Heating Method: Indirect

This hard, grainy textured cheese originally hails from the Parma, Reggio Emilia, Modena, Bologna, and Mantova provinces of Italy. A lengthy aging period is required to produce the grittiness and flavor characteristic of true Parmesan. Although its hard texture renders it ideal for grating, it is also delicious sliced and paired with fresh fruit and nuts as an after-dinner course. *Yield: Approximately 2 pounds*

YOU WILL NEED:

2 gallons skim or low-fat (2 percent) milk*

½ teaspoon (1 packet) direct-set thermophilic starter culture or 4 ounces fresh starter culture

4 ounces fresh starter culture

¼ teaspoon calcium chloride mixed with ¼ cup cold, sterilized water**

½ teaspoon liquid rennet (or ¼ tablet, crushed)

¼ cup cold, sterilized water

4 cups cheese salt or kosher salt

1 gallon cold water

*You can also use 1 gallon of skim or low-fat cow's milk and 1 gallon of whole goat's milk. This will result in a sharper flavored cheese.

**Omit if using raw milk.

Parmesan

TO PREPARE:

1. Warm the milk to 90°F (32°C) indirectly, using either a double boiler or a warm water bath (see page 65). Monitor the temperature of both the milk and the water bath using a dairy thermometer.

2. Add the starter culture and stir with a metal spoon to fully incorporate. Cover, and hold at 90°F (32°C) for 30 minutes.

3. Add the calcium chloride, if using, and stir for one minute. In a small bowl, whisk together the rennet and ¼ cup cold water. Slowly add the rennet solution to the milk mixture, and stir gently for one minute to fully incorporate. Cover again and allow to sit, maintaining the target temperature, for 30 minutes.

4. Check for a clean break. If curds cling to the cutting knife, allow them to sit and ripen for a bit longer. Once a clean break is achieved, cut the curds into ¼-inch cubes. Allow the cut curd to sit for five minutes.

5. Slowly heat the curd to 100°F (38°C). Do this very gradually, increasing the temperature only 1°F (-17°C) every one to three minutes. Stir frequently with a ladle, and gently cut any large pieces of curd that you may find.

6. Once you've reached 100°F (38°C), raise the temperature to 124°F (51°C). Stir the curd frequently. The curds should begin to shrink and reduce significantly in size. Remove the pot from the heat source, and allow the curds to rest for 10 minutes.

7. Ladle the curds out of the pot and into a 2-pound cheese mold lined with cheesecloth. If you are using a mold with an open bottom, place whatever you will be using as your drip pan underneath the cheese mold while you do this, so as to provide a solid base for the mold (otherwise, once you transfer the mold to the cheese press, your curd will spill out everywhere).

8. Once the curds are all ladled into the cheese mold, fold the excess cheesecloth over the top, place the follower in, and press the curd at 5 pounds of pressure for 15 minutes.

9. Take the cheese mold out of the press, remove the curd from the mold, and unwrap the cheesecloth. Change out the cheesecloth with a fresh, clean dressing, return the curd to the cheese mold, place the mold back into the cheese press, and press again at 5 pounds of pressure for another 30 minutes.

10. Repeat the process again, re-dressing the curd, and press at 15 pounds of pressure for two hours. Repeat one final time, re-dressing the curd, and press at 20 pounds of pressure for 12 to 14 hours.

11. Prepare a brine by dissolving the salt in 1 gallon cold water. Use a stainless-steel, glass, plastic, or ceramic container, as aluminum could corrode. Next, remove the curd from the mold, unwrap the cheesecloth, and submerge the curd in the brine. Allow to brine at room temperature for 24 hours.

12. Remove the curd from the brine, and pat dry. Place on a cheeseboard or cheese mat, and store in either a basement or a ripening refrigerator (see "Ripening Refrigerator" on page 35 for a discussion of home-ripening) at 50 to 55°F (10 to 13°C) and 85 percent humidity. Adjust the humidity, if necessary, by placing a bowl of warm water next to the cheese. Turn the cheese daily, and wipe with a dry cheesecloth or paper towel if any mold appears.

13. Store your cheese in this environment for six to 10 months. Monitor the humidity regularly, adding a bowl of warm water beside the cheese if needed. After the first month, turn the cheese weekly, continuing to remove any mold that appears with a dry cheesecloth or paper towel.

14. After two months, rub the surface of the cheese with a thin layer of olive oil. This will help prevent the rind from becoming too dry.

15. If you own a cheese trier, you can test the cheese at three months to see if the taste is to your liking. If you can wait, though, six to 10 months of aging will produce a much more intensely flavored Parmesan. Once it's ready, store the cheese in the refrigerator and use within one month.

Gorgonzola

Gorgonzola

Prep/Cook Time: 14 hours
Ripening Time: 3 days
Aging Time: 4 months
Heating Method: Indirect

Named after the small Italian town from which it originates, Gorgonzola is one of Italy's most beloved blue-veined cheeses. Salty, tart, pungent, and creamy, this crumbly cheese is equally delicious tossed with penne, crumbled over arugula, scattered atop pizza, or baked alongside fresh pears. The telltale blue lines found in Gorgonzola are the result of the mold *Penicillium roqueforti*, responsible for both the flavor and appearance of the cheese. In this recipe, you'll make one batch of curd, leave it to drain overnight, and then make a second batch the next morning.

Yield: Approximately 2 pounds

YOU WILL NEED:

- 2 gallons whole milk (cow's milk or goat's milk)
- 1 teaspoon (2 packets) direct-set mesophilic starter culture or 4 ounces fresh starter culture
- ¼ teaspoon calcium chloride mixed with ¼ cup cold, sterilized water*
- 1 teaspoon liquid rennet (or ½ tablet, crushed)
- ½ cup cold, sterilized water
- ¼ cup cheese salt or kosher salt, plus extra for sprinkling
- ⅛ teaspoon *Penicillium roqueforti*

  *Omit if using raw milk.

TO PREPARE:

1. Warm 1 gallon of the milk to 86°F (30°C) indirectly, using either a double boiler or a warm water bath (see page 65). Monitor the temperature of both the milk and the water bath using a dairy thermometer.

2. Add ½ teaspoon or 1 packet powdered starter culture (or 2 ounces, if using fresh) to the milk, and stir with a metal spoon to fully incorporate. Cover, and hold at 86°F (30°C) for 30 minutes.

3. Add the calcium chloride, if using, and stir for one minute. In a small bowl, whisk together half the rennet with ¼ cup cold water. Slowly add the rennet solution to the milk mixture, and stir gently for one minute to fully incorporate. Cover again and allow to sit, maintaining the target temperature, for 45 minutes.

4. Check for a clean break. If curds cling to the cutting knife, allow them to sit and ripen for a bit longer. Once a clean break is achieved, cut the curds into ½-inch cubes. Allow the cut curd to sit for 15 minutes.

5. Ladle the curds out of the pot and into a colander, drainer, or large sieve lined with a double layer of cheesecloth. Tie the four corners of the cheesecloth into a knot. Either hang the bag over a sink to drain, or place a wooden spoon or chopsticks through the knot and suspend the bag over a catch bowl. Allow the curds to drain overnight or until no whey is visibly dripping from the bag.

6. The next morning, repeat steps 1 through 5 with the second gallon of milk, leaving this batch of curd to drain for just one hour.

7. Remove the first batch of curd from the cheesecloth, cut into 1-inch cubes, and place in a bowl. Repeat with the new batch of curd, placing it in a separate bowl. Mix together the salt and *Penicillium roqueforti* in a third bowl. Disperse this mixture evenly over both bowls of curd. Carefully stir the salt/mold mixture into both batches of curd.

8. Add half of the newest batch of curd to a sterilized 2-pound cheese mold. Place the curd on the bottom and up the sides of the mold, leaving a depression in the center. Put all of the first batch of curd into that depression, and cover with the second half of the newer curd. It's entirely possible that you may end up with an extra bit of curd left over from both batches, unable to squeeze it all into the mold, so don't be alarmed if that occurs.

9. Place a clean cheeseboard on your countertop. Put a cheese mat on top of it, and then place the cheese mold in the center of the mat. Place a second cheese mat on top of the mold, and then top with a second cheeseboard. You will be flipping your cheese frequently over the next few days, and this setup makes turning the mold considerably easier.

10. Place the cheeseboard/mat/mold combination in a 55 to 60°F (13 to 16°C) environment, such as your basement or cheese fridge (see page 35). For the next two hours, flip the entire setup over every 15 minutes. I've found that placing the cheeseboard/mat/mold combination on a rack positioned over a 9 x 13-inch baking pan or dish is ideal for collecting the whey as it drains from the mold.

11. After two hours, place the cheeseboard/mat/mold combination in the 55 to 60°F (13 to 16°C) environment, making sure the humidity is at 85 percent. Keep it there for three days, flipping the apparatus over twice daily.

12. Take the cheese out of the cheese mold. Sprinkle salt over the entire surface of the cheese. Age at 55 to 60°F (13 to 16°C), with 85 percent humidity, for the next four days. Rub the entire surface with salt every day.

13. With the end of a sterilized ice pick or the tip of your dairy thermometer poke the cheese about 30 times, making sure to pierce all the way through the curd. Return the cheese to the 55 to 60°F (13 to 16°C) environment, with 85 percent humidity, and age for 30 days. During this time, the bacteria in the cheese will begin to grow and proliferate.

14. At the end of 30 days, move the cheese to a slightly colder area, around 50°F (10°C), still at 85 percent humidity. Leave to age in this environment for three months. Check the cheese every few weeks, scraping off any mold with a clean knife.

15. At the end of three months, your Gorgonzola is now ready to eat. Taste it and see if it is to your liking. If you prefer a stronger flavor, continue aging in the same environment, scraping off mold every few weeks, for another month or so. Once it is ready, store in the refrigerator and use within three weeks.

MAKING A HOMEMADE CHEESE PRESS

While it is entirely possible to purchase a fully constructed cheese press, it's actually quite easy to simply make your own. Furthermore, making a DIY cheese press, like crafting many things yourself, is considerably less costly. With a few simple steps, you can turn two cutting boards and some pipes into a lean, mean, pressing machine! When you're ready to press, don't forget to take the weight of the top cutting board into account.

Supplies & Materials

2 wooden cutting boards, each 1 inch thick, anywhere from 9 x 13 to 12 x 16 inches

4 galvanized pipes, each 18 inches long, with a 1/2-inch diameter

4 galvanized floor flanges for 1/2-inch pipe

16 wood screws, 3/4 inch

1 piece plywood or scrap board cut to the approximate size of the cutting boards

1 drip pan (You can purchase a metal drip pan from a cheese-making supplier as shown, or use an aluminum pie pan in which you've cut out a pouring spout.)

An assortment of weight-lifting plates, totaling 50 pounds (I use four 10-pound plates and one 5-pound plate; the remaining 5 pounds come from the weight of the cutting board itself.)

4 pipe end caps, if desired (for appearances only)

Tools

Electric drill

7/8-inch Forstner drill bit

11/2-inch Forstner drill bit

2 wood clamps

Drilling Frame Holes

1. Begin by placing the scrap board on a few soup cans or similar objects. The cans are necessary to add elevation, in order to accommodate the wood clamp.

2. Place one of the cutting boards on top of the scrap board. Line up the edges, and clamp the cutting board and the scrap board together. This will help to keep the drilled holes from splintering.

3. Using the 7/8-inch Forstner bit, drill holes in all four corners of the cutting board, so that the edge of the hole is 1 inch from the edge on each side of the corner. Be sure to drill all the way through the cutting board, but be careful not to drill through the scrap board. Remove the drilled cutting board and the scrap board from the cans. When assembled, this cutting board will be the bottom board of the cheese press.

4. Next, place the undrilled cutting board on the cans. Put the drilled cutting board on top of the undrilled cutting board, line up the edges, and clamp the boards together with the wood clamp.

5. Use the holes in the top board as guides for drilling into the bottom board. Using the 7/8-inch Forstner bit, drill just far enough to make a guide mark with the pointy center of the bit. Separate the boards.

6. Place the scrap board on top of the cans. Next, put the cutting board with the pilot holes on top of the scrap board and line up the edges, then clamp the two boards together firmly.

7. Following your pilot holes, drill holes through the cutting board with the 1 1/2-inch Forstner bit. When assembled, this will be the top board of the cheese press.

Attaching Pipes and Flanges
1. Attach the pipes to the flanges by turning each through the interior threads.

2. Slide the pipes through the cutting board with the 7/8-inch holes (the "bottom" board).

3. Next, attach four screws through the bottom of each flange up into the bottom of the cutting board. The flanges will serve as feet.

4. Standing upright, slide the pipes through the holes in the cutting board with the 1 1/2-inch holes (the "top" board).

5. Screw endcaps on if desired.

Assembling the Press
1. When you're ready to press some curd, lift the top cutting board up the pipes and off of the press.

2. Place your drip pan on the lower cutting board. Situate it so that the draining spout reaches to the edge of the cutting board.

3. Position a low-sided pan underneath the spout to serve as a catch tray for draining whey.

4. Place your curd-filled cheese mold, with its follower on top, on the drip pan. You'll need to put a "pusher" on top of the follower, to aid in compressing the curd. I use a pint-sized Mason jar with a plastic lid. A smaller cheese mold, fitted on top of the follower, works great, too.

5. Slide the top cutting board back over the pipes. Situate it evenly over your cheese mold/follower/pusher setup.

6. Add the amount of weight indicated in your recipe by placing the weight-lifting plates on top of the top cutting board. Be sure they are balanced squarely over the cheese mold. When calculating pressure, remember to account for the weight of the cutting board itself. The sheesham wood board used in my cheese press weighs 5 pounds.

The set-up | Detail | Curd in cheese cloth | Follower on top | Pusher atop Follower

Portrait of a Cheese-maker

Denise

When not tending to the needs of her toddler daughter, flock of chickens, or small herd of goats, Denise can be found crafting artisan cow's milk mozzarella. During a stint working in the wine and cheese department of a natural food store, she had the opportunity to learn a mozzarella-making technique from a seasoned Italian cheese-maker. After the birth of her daughter, Denise was looking for a skill (and schedule) she could juggle with her family's needs. Mozzarella-making seemed like a natural fit and a cottage-industry cheese-making business, Dee-Dee Lee's Cheese, was born. Using the commercial kitchen of a nearby business after hours, she makes her mozzarella once a week, and then sells it at a tailgate market, as well as at two local natural foods stores.

While making mozzarella is a livelihood for Denise, it's also an extension of her commitment to sustainable living. As she puts it, "I love the simplicity and complexity of it. It's natural, pure, and I can make it with my own two hands. I can be involved in the process from beginning to end, and no matter what, my cheese will be unlike anyone else's...completely unique. Ultimately, I make cheese to feel grounded, connected to the animals, the earth, and our sustainable culture." For newbie cheese-makers, Denise offers the following advice, honed from years of experience: "Don't cut corners, stay small, and don't give up." We'd all be wise to heed her words!

Portrait of a Cheese-maker

Cynthia

Cynthia got the home dairy-making itch back in 1983, when a successful attempt at making goat cheese wooed her forever. A former career as a job coach segued into a full-time gig as a dairy goat farmer and cheese-maker. Cynthia had always wanted goats, for their company as family pets as well as a source of milk for her then-young children. After acquiring several in the early 1980s, she decided they needed to "pay for themselves" and so began making cheese with the intention of selling it. She operated under the radar for a while, making what she calls "outlaw" cheese, but eventually became a fully legal cheese-maker.

These days, you'll find Cynthia fully immersed in all things goat. Her business, Oak Moon Farm & Creamery, specializes in raw-milk, aged, rustic, French-style goat cheeses. She also crafts a line of fresh herbed and flavored goat cheeses and blended chèvre specialties. In addition to making cheese almost daily for Oak Moon, she also prepares dairy items such as butter, kefir, and mozzarella for her family's use. Cynthia hosts several cheese-making workshops every year. The most frequent concerns she encounters amongst those just getting their dairy feet wet pertain to issues of safety and wasting milk. "I urge them not to fear their food, be smart and use good common sense, research and educate themselves in food handling and safety guidelines, and don't let the fear of failure keep them from making cheese. It may take a lot of trial and error and wasted milk to get the product you are looking for, so make friends with a dairy person!"

Chapter 7

Ice Cream:
Frozen Assets

With simply a bit of cream and sugar, it's possible to create homemade ice cream easily rivaling the more pricey pints found in your grocer's freezer aisle. In addition to saving money, you'll also save yourself from a litany of additives such as flavoring agents, stabilizers, and other chemicals used in the production of many commercially prepared ice creams. Best of all, the flavor possibilities are limitless, bound only by the riches of the season and the parameters of your imagination.

Basic Vanilla Ice Cream

Beginning with a simple vanilla ice cream recipe, it's possible to produce countless variations by the addition of an extra ingredient or two. The recipe offered here is about as simple as you'll find. Simply warm cream, add sugar and vanilla, and freeze. Ice cream machines offer varying instructions, so follow along with whatever is suggested by your model's manufacturer. *Yield: About 1 quart*

YOU WILL NEED:

- 4 cups heavy cream (or half-and-half for a less rich ice cream)
- ¾ cup granulated sugar
- 2 teaspoons vanilla extract

TO PREPARE:

1. Warm the cream in a medium saucepan over medium heat. Once small bubbles begin to appear around the edges of the cream, remove the pot from the heat and stir in the sugar. Keep stirring until the sugar is fully dissolved. Transfer the cream mixture to a glass or ceramic bowl and allow to cool slightly, then stir in the vanilla.

2. Cover the bowl and place it in refrigerator until completely chilled, four to six hours or overnight.

3. Add the chilled cream to the bowl of an ice cream maker, and process according to your model's instructions. When finished, you may either eat immediately (the ice cream will be rather soft at this point) or transfer to a freezable lidded container and store in the freezer.

SPRING

Strawberry, Chèvre & Balsamic Ice Cream

When strawberries make their triumphant late spring arrival, I can't get enough of them. Usually, I grab a handful right out of my strawberry patch and push as many of the sun-warmed nuggets into my mouth as will fit. While perfect unadorned, strawberries really shine when rendered into ice cream. This recipe introduces chèvre and balsamic vinegar, which help brighten the flavor and enhance the natural sweetness of the berries. *Yield: About 1 quart*

YOU WILL NEED:

- 1 cup strawberries, hulled and chopped
- 1 tablespoon balsamic vinegar
- ½ cup chèvre, crumbled or chopped into small pieces
- 1 recipe Basic Vanilla Ice Cream (above)

TO PREPARE:

1. Combine the strawberries and balsamic vinegar in a medium bowl. Toss until the fruit pieces are fully coated. Add the chèvre crumbles to the bowl, stirring gently.

2. Stir the strawberry-chèvre mixture into the ice cream mixture about halfway through the processing time, when the mixture just begins to freeze.

Ginger-Peach Ice Cream

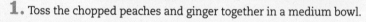

Is there any more fitting mascot for summer's plentiful abundance than a juicy, ripe, fragrant peach? For me, the most ideal, swoon-worthy offering wells up with juice, running down my chin and dripping onto my fingertips at the very first bite. Coupled with zesty, fiery crystallized ginger, this ice cream successfully alludes to summer's heat while cooling the palate. *Yield: About 1 quart*

YOU WILL NEED:

2 peaches, peeled and chopped

¼ cup crystallized ginger, finely chopped

1 recipe Basic Vanilla Ice Cream (page 105)

TO PREPARE:

1. Toss the chopped peaches and ginger together in a medium bowl.

2. Add the peach-ginger mixture to the ice cream mixture about halfway through the processing time, when the mixture just begins to freeze.

Spiced Apple Ice Cream

To me, the crispness of a fresh apple has always served as a direct correlate to the crispness of autumn air. Baked up with a bit of butter and a kiss of cinnamon and nutmeg, the sweet-tartness of these apples is a perfect foil to ice cream's rich creaminess. My favorite way of serving this dish is to toss some roasted and chopped walnuts or pecans on top, followed by a drizzle of local honey. Crisp, crunchy, sweet perfection! *Yield: About 1 quart*

YOU WILL NEED:

2 medium apples, peeled, cored, and chopped

2 tablespoons butter, melted

1 teaspoon ground cinnamon

½ teaspoon ground nutmeg

1 recipe Basic Vanilla Ice Cream (page 105)

TO PREPARE:

1. Preheat the oven to 375°F. Combine the apples, melted butter, cinnamon, and nutmeg in a medium bowl. Using clean hands or a wooden spoon, toss the ingredients together until the apples are fully coated in spices and butter.

2. Place the apple mixture on a small, greased, edged cookie sheet. Place in the preheated oven and bake for 20 minutes, until the apples have softened and are just slightly browned. Remove from the oven and allow to cool at room temperature.

3. Once the spiced apples have completely cooled, add them to the ice cream mixture about halfway through the processing time, when the mixture just begins to freeze.

Figgy Pudding Ice Cream

Dried fruits and warming spices are perfect wintertime delights. This ice cream brings to mind Victorian England with an unexpected twist on the beloved holiday dessert. A dash of rum or brandy, if you're so inclined, adds a festive touch. *Yield: About 1 quart*

YOU WILL NEED:

- 10 dried figs
- 6 fresh dates or ¼ cup dried dates, chopped
- 1 teaspoon ground cinnamon
- ¼ teaspoon ground nutmeg
- ½ teaspoon ground cloves
- ½ teaspoon ground allspice
- 2 tablespoons rum or brandy (optional; may also use rum flavoring)
- 1 recipe Basic Vanilla Ice Cream (page 105)

TO PREPARE:

1. Place the figs and dates in a medium bowl. Pour boiling water over the fruit, enough to fully cover. Allow them to rest until softened, two to three hours. Drain off liquid, and chop the fruit into small pieces. Return the fruit to the bowl.

2. Add the cinnamon, nutmeg, cloves, and allspice, and toss to combine. Add the rum or brandy, if desired, and stir thoroughly.

3. Add the spiced fruit to the ice cream mixture about halfway through the processing time, when the mixture just begins to freeze.

Portrait of a Dairy Lover

Kelly

A graphic designer by trade, Kelly's real labor of love is her lifestyle blog, www.eatmakeread.com. In it, she writes of her passion for creating good, whole, delicious foods, including dairy products. For the past few years, she has been crafting delectable dairy delights from the comfort of her urban kitchen and then posting recipes on her blog. Her most recent addition into food writing includes Remedy Quarterly, "a magazine filled with stories about food and recipes for feeling good."

Expanding on what she describes as "good cooking genes" inherited from her mother, Kelly finds continual inspiration for new culinary creations. That inspiration might come from ideas that arrive fully formed in her cook's mind's-eye, from a recipe happened upon in a magazine or online, or sometimes directly from the raw ingredients themselves. "Honestly, it's the farmers market that inspires me to make things. I absolutely love going there and connecting with the people who work so hard to provide my area with really amazing food."

To that end, Kelly encourages new home dairy-makers to "look to see if there are any local dairies in your area. The milk is so much fresher (and delicious) if you buy it from the source, and the people are always super friendly and willing to share recipe ideas with you. Also, be adventurous and try new things; it makes life more fun." As a prolific home dairy-maker of everything from butter to ice cream, frozen yogurt, popsicles, and a "panna cotta I made a while back that is so amazing and so easy it will just knock your socks off," it seems as though Kelly is exceptionally good at following her own advice!

Chapter 8
Recipes: Inspired Home Dairy Delights

You've learned how to whip up a creamery's worth of dairy products. Now, let's whisk that butter and tuck that Swiss into some enticing culinary creations! Whether you're looking for a way to render cream cheese into a tasty spread, a new way to serve eggs (with feta!), or an easy yogurt-based soup for days when it's much too hot to cook, you'll find a little bit of everything here.

Kefir Cornbread

Growing up in the southeast United States, cornbread was a regular component of many meals. Slathered in some homemade butter and served alongside a piping hot bowl of winter squash or lentil soup, I've long found cornbread a comfort food with few rivals.

Yield: 8 to 12 servings

YOU WILL NEED:

- 2 cups yellow cornmeal
- 1½ tablespoons sugar
- 2 teaspoons baking powder
- 1½ teaspoons baking soda
- 1 teaspoon salt
- 1 cup kefir
- 1 large egg
- 3 tablespoons unsalted butter, melted and cooled slightly

TO PREPARE:

1. Preheat the oven to 375°F (191°C). Butter an 8-inch square or 9-inch round baking pan, or a 10-inch cast iron skillet. Set aside.

2. Whisk together the cornmeal, sugar, baking powder, baking soda, and salt in a medium bowl.

3. Beat the kefir, egg, and butter with an electric mixer until well incorporated. At low speed, add in the dry ingredients until just blended, scraping down the sides of the bowl as needed. Be careful not to over mix as doing so can impair the cornbread's ability to rise.

4. Pour the batter into the prepared pan. Bake 30 to 35 minutes, until golden and firm. Remove from oven, and cool 15 minutes before serving.

Cucumber Yogurt Soup

YOU WILL NEED:

4 medium cucumbers, peeled, seeded, and chopped

2 cups plain yogurt

1 garlic clove, minced

3 tablespoons fresh dill, chopped

2 tablespoons fresh mint, chopped

2 tablespoons extra-virgin olive oil

1 tablespoon honey

Juice from ½ lemon

2 teaspoons ground cumin

1 teaspoon sea salt

1 teaspoon cracked black pepper

Naturally cooling cucumber, combined with yogurt, makes the ideal summer soup. Add a bit of mint and dill, and you've got an inherently refreshing starter. Best of all, everything goes straight into the food processor, so there's no need to heat up the kitchen. I love serving this with some smoked salmon and rye crisp crackers. Delicious!

Yield: 4 servings

TO PREPARE:

1. Combine the cucumber, yogurt, garlic, dill, mint, olive oil, honey, lemon juice, cumin, salt, and pepper in a large bowl. Puree in batches in a food processor or blender until uniformly smooth.

2. Serve the soup at once or store in a lidded container in the refrigerator, and use within two to three days.

Mac & Cheese

The ultimate comfort food, this grown-up version of a childhood favorite just might become your new favorite thing. The inclusion of just a hint of nutmeg and hot sauce provides a sophisticated layer of flavor. Paired with a side salad or sautéed broccoli, this easily works as an entrée.
Yield: 6 to 8 servings

TO PREPARE:

1. Preheat the oven to 350°F (177°C). Butter a 9 x 13-inch glass baking dish.

2. Cook the pasta until al dente, drain, and set aside in the prepared pan.

3. Meanwhile, add 2 tablespoons olive oil to a sauté pan, and heat the onion in the oil for five minutes. Add the garlic, and cook for an additional three minutes. Transfer the onion mixture to a small bowl, and set aside.

4. Add the flour and the remaining 3 tablespoons olive oil to the sauté pan. Cook over medium heat, stirring constantly, to make a blond roux.

5. Whisk the milk into the roux.

6. Add 2 cups cheese, and stir until smooth. Stir in the nutmeg, hot sauce, salt, and the reserved onion mixture. Separately, beat the eggs in a medium bowl. Stir the egg mixture into the cheese sauce.

7. Remove the sauce from the heat, and pour it over the pasta in the baking dish. Mix well. Top with remaining 1 cup cheese.

8. Bake for 30 minutes, until heated through and slightly browned on top. If you like it extra crispy on top, finish under the broiler for a minute or two.

Variation: To introduce a bit of autumn flavor, add baked apples and sage. Peel, core, and cube 4 medium apples and roast them at 350°F (177°C) for 30 minutes. Add the roasted apples, along with ½ cup of chopped fresh sage, to the roux in step 6.

YOU WILL NEED:

1 pound gobetti, or similar short, chunky pasta

1 medium onion, diced

5 tablespoons olive oil

2 garlic cloves, minced

3 tablespoons all-purpose flour

2 cups whole milk

3 cups grated cheddar cheese

½ teaspoon grated nutmeg

1 teaspoon hot sauce

Pinch of salt

4 large eggs

Saag Paneer

This dish is one of my most beloved Indian specialties. Garam masala (Hindi for "hot mixture") is a combination of different spices, varying regionally throughout India. It can be found at most natural and ethnic foods stores, as well as online through spice suppliers. Saag Paneer is perfect served with basmati rice, some garlic naan, and perhaps a fish or shrimp curry. *Yield: 4 servings*

YOU WILL NEED:

2 tablespoons ghee or butter

½ onion, finely chopped

2 tablespoons fresh ginger, peeled and minced

3 cloves garlic, minced

1 tablespoon garam masala

1 teaspoon turmeric

Salt

1 cup heavy cream

1 pound fresh spinach, washed and stemmed

1 pound paneer, cubed

½ cup tomatoes, chopped (optional)

Sea salt

TO PREPARE:

1. Melt the ghee in a large saucepan over medium heat. Add the onion, reduce the heat to low, and sauté for 10 minutes, stirring frequently to keep from sticking, until the onion becomes translucent and begins to brown slightly.

2. Add the ginger and garlic to the pan. Cook two minutes, stirring frequently, until the garlic is fragrant and begins to brown slightly. Add the garam masala, turmeric, and a pinch of salt, and stir well. Add the heavy cream and stir to thoroughly combine. Add the spinach. Cook for 20 minutes, stirring frequently, until the spinach is fully wilted and the sauce thickens.

3. Remove the pot from the heat. Puree the mixture with an immersion blender, or allow to cool slightly and then transfer contents to a food processor, and puree.

4. Return the mixture to the pan. Add the paneer and tomatoes, if using, and cook over low heat, stirring frequently, for five minutes, until heated through. Serve immediately.

Chèvre, Cranberry & Pecan Spread

Spread on crackers or raw vegetables, this appetizer is an instant classic for holiday gatherings. When served during cooler months, the ingredients showcase the best of winter's flavors. If you'd prefer not to include alcohol, simply replace the port wine with an equal amount of orange juice. *Yield: 10 to 12 servings*

YOU WILL NEED:

6 tablespoons (3 ounces) port wine

¼ cup maple syrup, divided

1 pound chèvre, at room temperature

2 tablespoons butter

½ cup pecan halves

Sea salt

¼ teaspoon cracked black pepper

½ cup dried cranberries

1 teaspoon fresh rosemary, chopped

TO PREPARE:

1. Heat the port in a small saucepan over medium heat until it has reduced to about half its volume. Stir in 2 tablespoons of the maple syrup. Remove from heat and allow to cool for five minutes.

2. Combine the cooled port mixture and the chèvre in a medium bowl, mixing until blended. Transfer the chèvre blend to a shallow serving dish, and spread evenly.

3. Melt the butter over low heat and then mix in the pecan halves. Add the remaining 2 tablespoons maple syrup, a pinch of salt, and the pepper. Cook for about two minutes, stirring frequently. Add the cranberries and rosemary, and cook for another minute. Remove the cranberry-pecan mixture from the heat, and let cool for five minutes.

4. Top the cheese evenly with the cranberry-nut mixture.

Shakshuka

A staple of North African cuisine, shakshuka consists of poached (or sometimes fried) eggs cooked in a blend of peppers, tomatoes, onions, and spices, adorned here with a generous sprinkling of feta. It is one of the most popular ways of serving eggs in my house. Light enough for breakfast yet satisfying as a dinner entrée if paired with salad and bread, shakshuka is the ideal anytime meal. *Yield: 4 servings*

YOU WILL NEED:

3 tablespoons olive oil	Red wine (optional)
1 red bell pepper, diced	Hot sauce (optional)
½ onion, diced	4 eggs
3 cloves garlic, minced	½ cup feta cheese
1 tablespoon ground cumin	3 tablespoons fresh cilantro or parsley, chopped
1 tablespoon paprika	
1 teaspoon ground coriander	Warm pita points or toast
Sea salt	
1 14-ounce can diced tomatoes	

TO PREPARE:

1. Warm the olive oil in a 12-inch sauté pan over medium low heat. Add the peppers and onion, and sauté for 10 minutes, stirring frequently, until the vegetables are softened and slightly browned.

2. Add the minced garlic, and cook for two minutes, until fragrant. Stir in the cumin, paprika, coriander, and a pinch of salt. Add the tomatoes, a splash of wine, and dash or two of hot sauce, if desired. Simmer for eight minutes, stirring frequently.

3. Carefully crack the eggs into the tomato mixture without breaking the yolks. Cover and cook for five minutes, until the eggs are set.

4. Remove the lid and sprinkle a small pinch of salt on the eggs. Sprinkle with the cilantro or parsley and the feta. Traditionally, it is served out of the pan on the table, with bread for scooping.

Swiss Cheese Fondue

Few dishes say "come in from the cold" like cheese fondue. This recipe includes a bit of hard apple cider and mustard for a truly autumnal feel. Served with toasted bread cubes and roasted vegetables, this dish works as either a robust appetizer for a crowd or a filling dinner for a few. For an alcohol-free version, simply replace the hard cider with an equal amount of fresh apple cider.

Yield: Serves 3 to 4

YOU WILL NEED:

1 pound grated Swiss cheese

2 tablespoons cornstarch

12 ounces hard apple cider

2 tablespoons grainy mustard

Grated nutmeg, if desired

TO PREPARE:

1. Toss the cheese with the cornstarch until thoroughly coated. Set aside.

2. Heat the hard cider in a large saucepan over medium-high heat until it reaches a near boil. Reduce the heat to low, and simmer for two minutes, until slightly reduced in volume. Start adding the cheese, one handful at a time, mixing it thoroughly as you go. Once all the cheese is incorporated, add the mustard and mix thoroughly.

3. Remove from the heat. Transfer the mixture to a fondue pot, if you have one. Alternately, you can cook the entire dish in the fondue pot. Serve with bite-sized lightly roasted vegetables and lightly toasted cubes of bread for dipping. If desired, top mixture with approximately 1/2 teaspoon freshly grated nutmeg.

If you've got an abundance of summer produce on your hands, this terrine is a tasty way to make the most of their combined flavors. Walnuts offer an unexpected element of crunchiness. Delicious paired with crusty bread and a robust glass of red wine. *Yield: 6 servings*

YOU WILL NEED:

- ¼ cup olive oil, divided
- 1 large yellow potato, cut into ½-inch slices
- 1 red bell pepper, seeded and cut into ½-inch strips
- 10 crimini mushrooms, cut into ¼-inch slices
- Sea salt, to taste
- 1 medium eggplant, peeled and sliced into eight ½-inch rounds
- 1 zucchini, cut into ¼-inch slices
- 1 24-ounce jar marinara sauce
- ¼ cup Parmesan cheese, grated
- 8 ounces fresh spinach
- 1 pound fresh mozzarella, grated
- 1 cup walnuts, chopped
- 1 tomato, sliced thinly

Roasted Vegetable & Mozzarella Terrine

TO PREPARE:

1. Preheat the oven to 400°F (204°C). Oil two baking sheets liberally with olive oil. Also, oil a 9 x 13-inch glass baking dish, and set aside.

2. In a medium bowl, toss the potato rounds, the pepper slices, and the mushrooms with 2 tablespoons olive oil until completely coated. Transfer to one of the prepared baking sheets in a single layer. Sprinkle the vegetables with salt, put the baking sheet in the preheated oven, and cook for 20 minutes.

3. Using the same mixing bowl, toss the eggplant and zucchini slices with the remaining 2 tablespoons olive oil until completely coated. Place the mixture on the second baking sheet, sprinkle with salt, and add to the oven with the first sheet.

4. After the first sheet has cooked for 20 minutes, remove, flip the potato slices, and return to the oven. Bake 10 minutes longer, and then remove both sheets. The vegetables will be softened, but not completely roasted at this point. Reduce the oven temperature to 375°F (191°C).

5. Spread one-third of the marinara sauce on the bottom of the glass baking dish. Layer the potato slices on top of the sauce, and sprinkle with half the grated Parmesan. Layer half of the spinach over the potato slices. Layer the eggplant slices over the spinach, followed by a layer of the zucchini slices. Cover with one-third of the sauce, sprinkle half of the mozzarella over the sauce, and then toss in the walnuts. Finish by layering the remaining spinach, Parmesan, mushrooms, peppers, and sauce. Sprinkle the remaining mozzarella on top, and cover with tomato slices.

6. Bake for 30 minutes, until the cheese is melted and bubbling. Let cool 10 minutes before eating.

This is my absolute favorite frosting. Making use of both homemade butter and cream cheese, it's the perfect blend of tangy, sweet, and citrusy notes. I've slathered it over everything from carrot cake to Earl Grey tea cupcakes. It would be delightful on scones, pound cake, or gingerbread, as well. *Yield: 3 cups*

YOU WILL NEED:

½ cup butter
1 cup cream cheese
1 teaspoon orange extract
Zest of 1 orange
3 cups confectioner's sugar

TO PREPARE:

1. Beat the butter and cream cheese with an electric mixer at low speed until fully incorporated. Beat in the orange extract and zest, stopping the mixer to scrape down the sides with a spatula as necessary.

2. Add the confectioner's sugar, and beat on low speed until the mixture is smooth. Increase the speed to medium, and beat for two minutes until fluffy and uniformly smooth.

3. Spread liberally on your dessert of choice!

Variation: Vanilla Cream Cheese Frosting: This frosting works equally well without orange zest or extract. Simply omit the zest, and substitute an equal amount of vanilla extract for the orange extract.

Orange Cream Cheese Frosting

The lighter cousin to its cream cheese-based kin, ricotta cheesecake is perfect for those (like me!) who love cheesecake but are daunted by its richness. Lemon zest, cinnamon, and vanilla provide the most delicate of flavors. I love serving this drizzled with a bit of local honey and a handful of pomegranate seeds alongside a glass of port in winter, or topped with fresh, crushed berries and a flute of sparkling wine during warmer months. *Yield: 8 servings*

YOU WILL NEED:

2 pounds ricotta cheese

6 large eggs, at room temperature

¾ cup granulated sugar

¼ cup all-purpose flour

1 tablespoon vanilla extract

1 tablespoon lemon zest

½ teaspoon ground cinnamon

¼ teaspoon sea salt

TO PREPARE:

1. Preheat the oven to 300°F (149°C). Butter and flour a 9 ½-inch springform pan, and set aside.

2. Combine the ricotta, eggs, sugar, flour, vanilla, lemon zest, cinnamon, and salt in a large mixing bowl. Using a whisk, beat until thoroughly incorporated.

3. Pour the batter into the prepared pan. Bake 1 ½ hours, until the top is golden and the cake is puffy. Insert a sharp knife or cake tester. If the cheesecake is done, the knife will come out clean. Otherwise, return to the oven for an additional seven minutes, and test again.

4. Cool on a wire rack. The cheesecake will deflate a bit as it cools. Serve immediately, or cover and chill in the refrigerator until ready.

Ricotta Cheesecake

Chapter 9

Body Care:
The Land of Milk & Honey

The use of dairy products in personal care is nothing new. Cleopatra's milk baths are the stuff of legends. Queens Elizabeth I of England and Elisabeth of Bavaria are said to have dabbled in dairy, as well. From whole cow's milk to goat-milk yogurt and beyond, dairy products have been incorporated into body care regimens for probably as long as animals have been domesticated. While you're crafting up dairy delights for whetting the appetite, you can simultaneously satiate your skin's need for moisture. Dual-purpose dairy to the rescue!

THE MAGIC OF MILK

A number of different qualities present in milk products have restorative effects on skin. Most notable among them is lactic acid, a type of alpha hydroxy acid that is most readily found in cultured dairy products. Alpha hydroxy acids (or "AHAs") are known for their ability to penetrate and loosen up the upper-most layers of skin cells. As a result, a natural shedding process begins. The skin releases dead cells, letting newly formed cells rise to the surface and promoting collagen production. The appearance of fresh skin cells reduces visible signs of aging, such as wrinkles and damage caused by sun exposure. Lactic acid is an AHA overachiever. Not only is it known for its ability to deeply hydrate, it also is a top-tier exfoliant.

Lactic acid-rich dairy products such as yogurt, buttermilk, sour cream, kefir, and cultured butter are wonderfully enriching and moisturizing to skin. By incorporating these homemade dairy products into your skin care routine, you'll soften and clear out old skin debris gently. Lactic acid products are therefore ideal for those with sensitive skin (like me!), who are especially susceptible to irritation and damage from harsher AHAs, such as glycolic acid (commonly used in facial peels).

In addition to lactic acid, milk contains vitamins, minerals, enzymes, fats, and proteins that benefit the skin. The calcium, vitamin A, and vitamin E in milk and milk products help the skin to look refreshed and rested, while fats and proteins work to smooth and hydrate. The saturated fat found in whole milk (the milk of choice used in body care products prepared both commercially and for home use) coats the skin in an emollient-rich wash, allowing damaged or aging skin to regain a bit of moisture and plumpness. In the following recipes, either whole cow or goat's milk will work equally well. Please note that the measurements in each recipe provide enough for one use, except for "A Sight for Sore Eyes Mask," which yields two uses.

FACE

In the Clear Facial Cleanser

Kefir and aloe play off of each other here to simultaneously soothe, heal, clean, and nourish the skin. Honey—which contains trace amounts of naturally occurring hydrogen peroxide—kills off bacteria and works to gently clear up any surface blemishes or areas of inflammation. *Yield: 1 use*

YOU WILL NEED:

- 3 tablespoons aloe vera gel*
- 3 teaspoons plain kefir
- 1 tablespoon raw honey

  *Aloe vera gel may be purchased at your local natural food store or drug store or by squeezing the gel out of an aloe vera plant.

TO PREPARE:

1. Place the aloe vera gel, kefir, and honey in a small bowl. Using a fork or small whisk, blend until fully incorporated.

2. Apply the cleanser to the face using your fingertips or a cotton ball. Be sure to keep away from your eyes. I usually just gently tap some cleanser in a wide circle with my fingertips around the outer edges of the entire eye area.

3. Massage the cleanser into the skin in a gentle circular motion. Rinse thoroughly with warm water, and lightly pat your skin dry.

Tighten & Lighten Face Mask

While sour cream might not be the first ingredient you think of for body care, it's certainly an option worthy of serious consideration. As a cultured dairy product, sour cream is rich in lactic acid. When blended with honey and egg white, sour cream works synergistically to clean pores, slough off dead skin cells, and deeply moisturize the skin. Both bergamot and geranium essential oils offer the double punch of combating inflammation while offering up a delightful fragrance. *Yield: 1 use*

YOU WILL NEED:

- 3 tablespoons whole milk sour cream
- 1 tablespoon raw honey
- 1 egg white
- 2 drops bergamot essential oil
- 2 drops geranium essential oil

TO PREPARE:

1. Place the sour cream, honey, egg white, and essential oils in a medium bowl. Whisk thoroughly until well combined.

2. Apply the mixture to a clean face in upward strokes with fingertips. Take care to keep away from the eye-socket area.

3. Allow the mask to dry for 15 to 20 minutes. Wash your face clean with warm water, and pat dry gently with a towel.

Squeaky Clean Facial Scrub

Almond meal is an ideal choice for a scrub, as it offers a gentle exfoliant packed with vitamins, minerals, and beneficial oils. Paired up with yogurt, honey, and a bit of orange juice for beneficial alpha hydroxy fruit acids, this scrub will simultaneously cleanse, exfoliate, and soften. *Yield: 1 use*

YOU WILL NEED:

- 4 teaspoons ground almond meal
- 3 teaspoons whole milk yogurt
- 2 teaspoons fresh orange juice
- 1 teaspoon raw honey

TO PREPARE:

1. Combine the almond meal, yogurt, orange juice, and honey in a small bowl. Using a fork or small whisk, mix until well combined.

2. Apply the scrub to the face with fingertips. Rub into the skin with a circular motion for one to two minutes, taking care to avoid the eye area. Rinse thoroughly with warm water.

A Sight for Sore Eyes Mask

The skin around your eyes has special needs. Eye-socket skin is actually the thinnest on your entire face, requiring the gentlest of touches. It also contains lymph glands that, unless stimulated, retain metabolic wastes. Your eyes and the skin around them reflect a good deal about your state of health. If you're tired, ill, lacking nutrients, or dehydrated, your eyes will show it. In this nourishing mask, sour cream works to remove dead skin cells and decrease wrinkles, while green tea, a natural diuretic, reduces puffiness and swelling while increasing blood flow. A dash of rose hip seed oil introduces healing vitamin C and essential fatty acids. **Yield: 2 uses**

YOU WILL NEED:

2 tablespoons sour cream

1 tablespoon brewed green tea

½ teaspoon rose hip seed oil

TO PREPARE:

1. Place the sour cream, tea, and rose hip seed oil in a small bowl. Using a fork or small whisk, blend until fully incorporated.

2. Apply the cream to the eye area with fingertips. Maintain a ¼-inch border around the eye socket area to prevent migration into the eye itself.

3. Keep the mask on for 30 minutes. Rinse gently with warm water, and use a soft cloth to remove excess. Pat the eye area gently with a dry cloth. Store the remaining eye mask mixture in the refrigerator, and use within one week.

Dog Days of Summer Conditioner

Summer is famous for bikinis, boardwalks, and bad hair, or, at least, it long ago established such a reputation with me. To combat the dry, crunchy tresses brought on by summer sun, seawater, and chlorine, I turn to a time-honored combination of yogurt and bananas. Lactic acid in the yogurt helps remove surface debris accumulated on the scalp. Bananas are packed with potassium, tryptophan, and vitamins A, B, C, and E, all of which combine to imbue the hair with abundant moisture, pliability, and sheen. Citrus essential oils impart a cheering and uplifting aroma reminiscent of summertime fun. **Yield: 1 use**

YOU WILL NEED:

- 1 ripe banana
- ⅓ cup whole milk yogurt
- 2 tablespoons raw honey
- 1 egg, beaten
- 4 drops tangerine, orange, or grapefruit essential oil

TO PREPARE:

1. Place the banana, yogurt, honey, egg, and essential oil in a blender or food processor. Blend until thoroughly combined.

2. To use, wet your hair and apply the conditioner. Massage the mixture into the scalp, and rub through with fingers to tips. Place either a plastic shower cap or towel on your head, and leave the conditioner on for 20 minutes. The heat created by covering the head allows the mixture to more fully penetrate the scalp and hair.

3. Rinse your hair thoroughly with warm water. Shampoo and style your hair as usual.

Winter's Grasp Dry Scalp Mask

The harsh climatic conditions of winter can exact just as heavy of a toll on hair as summertime sun and fun. Low humidity coupled with strong winds can dry out the scalp and mane alike. Introduce some moisture via avocados and sour cream. Avocados are naturally high in healthy fats and full of nourishing fat-soluble vitamins E and K. Lather this mask on, relax in a hot bath while it works its magic, and stave off the ravages of winter in both body and soul! **Yield: 1 use**

YOU WILL NEED:

- 1 avocado, pitted and mashed
- ¼ cup whole milk sour cream
- 1 tablespoon extra-virgin olive oil

TO PREPARE:

1. Place the avocado, sour cream, and olive oil in a food processor or blender, and puree until smooth.

2. To use, wet your hair and apply the mixture. Massage the mixture into your scalp, and rub through with fingers to tips. Run a fine-toothed comb through your hair to evenly distribute the mixture. Place either a plastic shower cap or a towel on your head, and leave the conditioner on for 20 minutes. The heat created by covering the head allows the mixture to more fully penetrate the scalp and hair.

3. Rinse thoroughly with warm water. Shampoo and style your hair as usual.

Tropical Refresher Body Scrub

Every body needs some love sometime. Nothing beats a good scrub for getting the blood circulating, smoothing the skin, and providing moisture from head to toe. The lactic acid in kefir works to gently exfoliate, while lime and sea salt draw out toxins and soften up rough patches. **Yield: 1 *use***

YOU WILL NEED:

- 1 cup sea salt
- ¾ cup kefir
- Juice of 2 limes
- 2 tablespoons extra-virgin olive oil
- 2 drops lime essential oil (optional)
- 2 drops lemon essential oil (optional)
- 2 drops grapefruit essential oil (optional)

TO PREPARE:

1. Place the salt, kefir, lime juice, olive oil, and essential oils in a medium bowl. Using a fork or small whisk, blend until fully incorporated. Transfer to a lidded jar, refrigerate, and use within 3 days.

2. To use, apply to the body with fingertips while showering. Massage into the skin with a gentle circular motion. Rinse thoroughly with warm water, and lightly pat dry with a towel. You might want to give your shower or tub a scrubbing afterwards, so that the next person doesn't encounter a slick floor.

Cleopatra's Secret Bath Soak

Egypt's notorious kohl-rimmed queen was known for her beauty as much as her controversial rule (and love life!). Undoubtedly her milk baths contributed to her legendary looks. Long regarded as a fast train to beautiful skin, the proteins in milk and buttermilk work to dissolve dead skin cells. Add a touch of honey, pair it with the captivating aroma of geranium and bergamot, and your rightful place as the ruler of your domain will go unchallenged. **Yield: 1 *use***

YOU WILL NEED:

- 3 cups whole milk buttermilk
- 2 tablespoons raw honey
- 1 tablespoon jojoba, sweet almond, or grapeseed oil
- 5 drops bergamot essential oil
- 5 drops geranium essential oil

TO PREPARE:

1. Gently warm the buttermilk, either on the stovetop or in a microwave. Heat just until it is warm to the touch, not all the way to boiling. If the buttermilk is comfortably warm on your fingertips, that's perfect. Add the honey, oil, and essential oils, and whisk until fully incorporated.

2. To use, fill a bath with warm water. Add the buttermilk mixture to the bath. Using your hand, stir the water until the mixture is fully dispersed. Soak as long as the water remains at a comfortable temperature. Rinse off with warm water, and gently pat dry with a towel.

A Show of Hands **Hand Mask**

Our hands take lots of abuse: From calluses caused by rigorous yard work to cracks and cuts brought on by dishwashing and winter weather. Give them a restorative treatment to bring back moisture and aid in healing. They're one of our most relied-on body parts, so it's time they received the loving care they deserve. *Yield: 1 use*

YOU WILL NEED:

- 3 tablespoons whole milk yogurt
- 1 teaspoon jojoba, sweet almond, or grapeseed oil
- 2 drops lavender essential oil (optional)

TO PREPARE:

1. Combine the yogurt, oil, and essential oil in a small bowl. Using a fork or small whisk, mix until well combined.

2. To use, massage the mixture into your hands. Leave on for 30 minutes or until mixture is fully dry. Rinse off, and then apply a thick, emollient cream to lock in moisture. Alternatively, cover hands with lightweight cotton gloves and leave on overnight. Rinse off and follow with hand cream in the morning.

Walkin' on Sunshine **Foot Scrub**

I don't know about you, but I'm a habitual foot abuser. I rely on my feet to do most everything, seldom offering them any sort of respite. That's where this scrub comes in. By slathering them in a buttery rub, I'm able to simultaneously slough off rough spots and imbue them with softness. In no time, I've added an extra spring to my step, and so can you. *Yield: 1 use*

YOU WILL NEED:

- ½ cup butter, at room temperature*
- ½ cup brown sugar
- 3 drops rosemary, peppermint, or spearmint essential oil (optional)

  *Cultured or whipped butter or ghee all work equally well.

TO PREPARE:

1. Place the butter, sugar, and essential oil in a medium bowl. Using a fork or small whisk, blend until fully incorporated. You can use a food processor or blender instead, if you prefer.

2. To use, apply the butter to your feet and massage gently, rubbing in between toes and on soles, as well. Remove thoroughly with warm water in the bath or shower and then lightly pat feet dry. You might want to give your shower or tub a scrubbing afterwards, so that the next person doesn't encounter a slick floor.

Raw Honey

In many recipes in this chapter, I call for "raw" honey. This is honey in its unprocessed form, exactly as it came out of the extractor. Much of the honey available commercially has been heated and filtered. This is done to make it appear more smooth and clean. In heating honey, however, many of its inherent fragile (and subtle) aromas, enzymes, beneficial yeasts, and other nutrients are destroyed. Heated honey is therefore not as nutritious as raw honey, whether used internally or externally. Examine the label on your honey bottle. If it doesn't say "raw," "unfiltered," "unheated," or "unprocessed," it has been heat-processed.

Portrait of a Milk Soap-maker

Tina

Tina knows just what it takes to look good: goats. She adds locally sourced goat's milk to several of the soaps made by her business, Faerie Made. Along with body care products and botanical perfumes, Tina makes more than 20 different types of soaps, several of which feature a goat's-milk base.

"What began as a hobby over a decade ago has morphed into a full-scale business. Tina now makes products, including her goat's-milk soaps several times every month. She discovered early on the creaminess imparted by goat's milk. **"I love what goat's milk gives to soap."** The success of her business and the efficacy of her products reinforce to me the notion that milk really does do a body good—both inside and out.

Resources

Metric Conversion Chart by Volume (for Liquids)

U.S.	Metric (milliliters/liters)
¼ teaspoon	1.25 mL
½ teaspoon	2.5 mL
1 teaspoon	5 mL
1 tablespoon	15 mL
¼ cup	60 mL
½ cup	120 mL
¾ cup	180 mL
1 cup	240 mL
2 cups (1 pint)	480 mL
4 cups (1 quart)	960 mL
4 quarts (1 gallon)	3.8 L

Cooking Measurement Equivalents

3 teaspoons = 1 tablespoon
2 tablespoons = 1 fluid ounce
4 tablespoons = ¼ cup
5 tablespoons + 1 teaspoon = ⅓ cup
8 tablespoons = ½ cup
10 tablespoons + 2 teaspoons = ⅔ cup
12 tablespoons = ¾ cup
16 tablespoons = 1 cup
48 teaspoons = 1 cup
1 cup = 8 fluid ounces
2 cups = 1 pint
2 pints = 1 quart
4 quarts = 1 gallon

Metric Conversion Chart by Weight (for Dry Ingredients)

U.S.	Metric (grams/kilograms)
¼ teaspoon	1 g
½ teaspoon	2 g
1 teaspoon	5 g
1 tablespoon	15 g
16 ounces (1 pound)	450 g
2 pounds	900 g
3 pounds	1.4 kg
4 pounds	1.8 kg
5 pounds	2.3 kg
6 pounds	2.7 kg

Temperature Conversion

Fahrenheit	Celsius
32°	0°
212°	100°
250°	121°
275°	135°
300°	149°
350°	177°
375°	191°
400°	204°
425°	218°

MAIL-ORDER SUPPLIERS

Cheese molds, cheese presses, cultures, mold powders, lipase, rennet, and beyond

CANADA

Glengarry Cheesemaking
and Dairy Supply Ltd.
888-816-0903
www.glengarrycheesemaking.on.ca

UNITED KINGDOM

Ascott Smallholding Supplies, Ltd.
0845-130-6285
www.ascott.biz

Moorlands Cheesemakers
0174-985-0108
www.cheesemaking.co.uk

Smallholder Supplies
0147-687-0070
www.smallholdersupplies.co.uk

UNITED STATES

Caprine Supply
913-585-1191
www.caprinesupply.com

Hoegger Supply Company
800-221-4628
www.hoeggergoatsupply.com

Leeners
800-543-3697
www.leeners.com

Lehman's
888-438-5346
www.lehmans.com

New England Cheesemaking
Supply Company
413-628-3808
www.cheesemaking.com

The Beverage People
800-544-1867
www.thebeveragepeople.com

The Cheesemaker
414-745-5483
www.thecheesemaker.com

Live Kefir Grains

Happy Herbalist
888-425-8827
www.happyherbalist.com

Raw Milk

A Campaign for Real Milk
202-363-4394
www.realmilk.com/where.html

Spices and Herbs

Frontier Natural Products Co-op
800-669-3275
www.frontiercoop.com

Penzeys Spices
800-741-7787
www.penzeys.com

Simply Organic
800-437-3301
www.simplyorganicfoods.com

Vinegar

Eden Organic
888-424-3336
www.edenfoods.com

Bragg Health Products
800-446-1990
www.bragg.com

Spectrum
800-434-4246
www.spectrumorganics.com

PERIODICALS

The following publications often contain useful information on home dairy-making:

BackHome
www.backhomemagazine.com

Countryside & Small Stock Journal
www.countrysidemag.com

Creamline
www.smalldairy.com/publications.
html

Culture
www.culturecheesemag.com

Grit
www.grit.com

Hobby Farm Home
www.hobbyfarms.com/hobby-farm-home-portal.aspx

Mother Earth News
www.motherearthnews.com

Urban Farming
www.hobbyfarms.com/urban-farm/urban-farm.aspx

A NOTE FROM THE AUTHOR: It takes a good bit of time for a book to make its way from initial idea to printed copy. That means that as helpful as a list like this one is, by the time you're holding your book in your hands, it's inevitable that some of the websites or contact information will have changed and that useful new resources will have surfaced. Still, it's a great starting point for those just entering the world of all things dairy. And about those changes and updates? I'm tracking them all in a regularly updated Resources section of my blog. Be sure to visit me regularly there: www.small-measure.blogspot.com.

Glossary

Acidity. Introduced via starter culture or an acidifying agent (such as vinegar), acidity refers to the percentage of lactic acid present in a dairy product at varying stages in its production. Acidity levels differ between milk, whey, and curd as a product ages. Also refers to the amount of tartness or sourness in a dairy product.

Aging. Also known as "ripening," aging is used to develop flavor and texture in cheese-making. Refers to the length of time cheese is held at a specific temperature and humidity level. Fresh cheeses are, by definition, not aged.

Annatto. Produced from the reddish-tinted pulp that surrounds seeds of achiote tree fruit, annatto is used to color everything from cheese to margarine and even lipstick. It mimics the yellow that would otherwise be found in the milk of grass-fed cows.

Ash. Derived from dried salt and vegetables, ash creates a hospitable environment for surface mold growth, desirable in certain cheeses. Adding ash, an alkaline substance, works to neutralize the acidity found in cheese, which might otherwise slow down ripening and, consequently, flavor development.

Brevibacterium linens. A red mold, used to create orange and yellow coloration on cheese surfaces. Often referred to as "red cultures," it develops quickly, assisting with ripening. The sulphurous aromas produced by the mold are characteristic of brick, Limburger, and Muenster cheeses.

Brining. The process of submerging cheese in a solution of salt and water. In cheese-making, brining helps flavor to develop, rinds to form, and bacterial growth to be curtailed.

Casein. The primary protein found in milk. Casein coagulates not via heat, but through its interaction with rennet and acids. Its presence in milk is responsible for importing structure to cheeses.

Calcium Chloride. A liquid solution used in cheese-making when working with pasteurized and homogenized milk. Such processes impair the ability of rennet to properly coagulate when making cheese. Calcium chloride permits the formation of a firmer curd. Not necessary when working with raw milk.

Cheddaring. A style of cheese-making, named after the village of Cheddar in Somerset County, England, from which the cheese originated. The process of cheddaring refers to kneading curd with salt after heating and draining off whey. The curds are then cut into blocks, which are stacked onto one another and turned repeatedly until any remaining moisture is pressed out and a firm curd results.

Cheese Wax. Assists in preventing hard cheeses from drying out during aging. This type of wax is made especially for use in cheese-making and is deliberately soft and pliant. In addition to preventing dryness and brittleness, wax also keeps harmful bacteria out of cheese while it is ripening.

Cheese Press. Necessary when making hard cheeses, cheese presses work by applying continued pressure onto curds that have been placed into a mold. The pressure squeezes whey from the curds, forming them into a solid mass.

Cheese Salt. Flake, or cheese-making, salt is a coarse, non-iodized salt that completely dissolves in water, leaving behind no grit, grains, or residue of any kind. Iodine can kill off important cheese cultures, as well as slow down the aging process. Cheese salt is available from cheese-making suppliers; you can also use kosher or canning salt with equal success.

Cheese Trier. A tool used by cheese-makers to sample a bit of cheese from the center of a wheel to test for ripeness. Made of stainless steel and used only when making hard cheeses, the trier lets a cheese-maker check on where their cheese is at in its aging process without having to cut a wedge out of the wheel itself.

Cheese Mat. Similar in use to cheese-boards, cheese, or "drying," mats are made of bamboo or food-grade plastic. These mats are necessary for draining cheeses such as Brie, Camembert, and Coulommiers, and also aid in the aging and air-drying process following pressing.

Cheese Molds. Used for forming curds into specific shapes, cheese molds are utilized in the final stages of cheese-making and determine the ultimate shape of a cheese. From rounds to pyramids, columns to hearts, molds come in a variety of shapes and sizes. Commercially purchased cheese molds are made from wood, stainless steel, ceramic, and food-grade plastic.

Clean Break. This refers to the state of curds when they are ready to be cut. When the curds reach the correct stage, they will break cleanly and evenly when either a thermometer, curd knife, or finger is inserted into them.

Cheesecloth. As its name implies, cheesecloth was originally used to wrap cheeses for preserving. While still used for this purpose, depending on the cheese being made, it is more routinely used to drain whey from curds and for lining cheese molds intended for hard cheeses.

Coagulation. This is the process by which milk becomes thickened, firm, and custard-like. Coagulation occurs due to interaction between milk and either rennet or an acid. Necessary for the development of curd.

Cultured. Cultured dairy products are, by definition, those that have undergone fermentation. See Fermentation.

Curd. The solid, coagulated mass formed in milk through the interaction of rennet and bacterial cultures. Curd is largely comprised of milk protein and fat.

DVI/Direct Set Cultures. Laboratory-born cultures containing all of the important characteristics found in traditionally made cultures without the need to first be cultured. Available in powdered form and stored in the freezer until needed, direct-set cultures are simply added to warmed milk. Many come in single-use packages, intended to work in 2 gallons of milk.

Drying. A process used to form rind on some cheeses. Drying, or "air drying," aids in protecting the interior of cheeses during the sometimes lengthy aging process.

Fermentation. When applied to foods, fermentation refers to the transformation of carbohydrates into alcohols and carbon dioxide (as well as other organic acids), on account of the presence of yeast and bacteria. During dairy fermentation, bacteria found in milk and air interact, turning milk sugar (or "lactose") into lactic acid. The bacteria responsible for this conversion can include *Streptococcus, Lactobacillus, Lactococcus,* and *Leuconostoc.*

Geotrichum candidum. Used in conjunction with other molds, *Geotrichum candidum* contributes to both flavor and physical integrity during the ripening process of cheeses such as Brie and Camembert. It is also used in ripening for some goat cheeses. The mold aids in creating a neutral environment in which *Penicillium candidum* and *Brevibacterium linens* can flourish.

Heavy Cream. Defined in the United States as cream with a fat content between 30 and 40 percent. Also called *whipping cream* or *heavy whipping cream.*

Homogenization. The process used to combine two insoluble substances into an emulsion. Homogenization punctures the butterfat particles in milk. These particles are then made small enough to no longer separate from the water found in milk, creating a uniformly distributed product.

Lactic Acid. An acid formed during dairy fermentation. Bacteria present in the milk and air consume milk sugar (or "lactose"), transforming it into lactic acid.

Lactose. The naturally occurring sugar found in milk. Lactose comprises anywhere between two and eight percent of milk's total weight, varying between species and individuals.

Lipase. A type of enzyme made by certain animals (including humans) that breaks down dietary fats during digestion. In the home dairy, the role of lipase is to impart certain types of cheeses with their characteristic strong flavors. Coupled with ripening time, lipase provides the nuanced flavors that distinguish certain cheeses.

Mesophilic Starter. This form of starter culture is considered "non-heat loving," meaning it doesn't do well if heated beyond 103°F (39°C). Mesophilic cultures are used to make cheeses preferring low milk and curd temperatures, such as Gouda, cheddar, and feta.

Milling. A step in the cheese-making process. Curds are broken or torn up into smaller, irregular pieces before being placed into a mold and pressed.

Mold-ripened cheese. A type of cheese to which a specific mold has been added and encouraged to proliferate. Molds are added either internally, as in the case of blue molds, or externally, for white mold cheeses such as Brie and Camembert.

Pasteurization. Named after French chemist and biologist Louis Pasteur, pasteurization is a process that greatly slows the growth of microbes in food. First performed in 1862, pasteurization curtails the number of pathogens likely to cause disease in foods, permitting that a product, once pasteurized, is refrigerated and consumed in an expedient manner. The process kills all bacteria in milk, which is why it is necessary to add starter culture to milk that has undergone pasteurization.

Penicillium camemberti. This white mold is quite similar to *Penicillium candidum*, producing many parallels in characteristic flavor and appearance. *Penicillium camemberti*, however, is used more often in producing goat's milk (as opposed to cow's milk) soft cheeses.

Penicillium candidum. A white mold used to ripen Brie, Camembert (made with cow's milk), Coulommiers, Sainte-Maure, and some French-style goat cheeses. After it is sprayed onto the surface of the curd, it spreads and grows incredibly quickly, keeping other molds from developing in the process. It is then allowed to age, during which time its characteristic white bloomy rind forms. Also contributes to the development of flavor during the ripening stage.

Penicillium roqueforti. A type of blue mold. Found in Stilton, Roquefort, Gorgonzola, Danablu, and other blue cheeses, the mold imparts the characteristic blue-green ripple typical of such cheeses,

along with a smooth, creamy, spreadable texture. Enzymes found in *Penicillium roqueforti* are responsible for producing the pleasingly pungent flavor and aroma associated with blue cheeses. These enzymes cause the mold to grow inside of the curds, breaking down complex molecules into simple ones, changing the fibrous chemical structure into a smoother one, and imbuing it with piquant flavor and smell.

Pressing. A step in cheese-making in which pressure is applied to curds that have been added to cheesecloth-lined molds. Pressing allows any excess whey to be removed from the curds. It also causes the curds to meld into one another, producing one continuous mass. Variations in applied pressure are based on curd size and intended texture.

Proprionic shermanii. A white mold responsible for putting the holes (or "eyes"), smell, and taste into Swiss, Emmentaler, and Gruyère cheeses.

Raw Milk. Milk that has not been subjected to any processing whatsoever. Raw milk possesses a number of qualities that are otherwise destroyed or reduced during pasteurization and Homogenization, including beneficial bacteria (such as lactic acids), heat-sensitive enzymes (including lactase, lipase, and phosphatase), and vitamins A, B_6, and C (all heat-sensitive nutrients).

Rennet. A collection of naturally occurring enzymes, rennet is found in the stomach of any mammal, and is used in digesting mother's milk. One proteolytic (protein-digesting) enzyme in particular, chymosin (or rennin) coagulates milk,

separating curds, or solids, from whey, the liquid portion of milk. Helpful in mammals for digestion, the role of rennet is equally important in cheese-making.

Rind. The outermost layer of a cheese. Cheese rind is formed as the surface dries during aging. Harder than the interior, the rind works to seal in both moisture and flavor. While many rinds are edible, consuming them is often a matter of personal preference.

Ripening. Also known as "aging," ripening is used to develop flavor and texture in cheese-making. Refers to the length of time cheese is held at a specific temperature and humidity level. Fresh cheeses are, by definition, not ripened.

Salting. A step in cheese-making in which non-iodized flake salt is added to curd. This is often done at the time of milling, before molding or pressing. Salt is also sometimes added to the surface of finished cheeses.

Starter Culture. Bacterial cultures that consume lactose, or milk sugar, giving off lactic acid as a by-product. Lactic acid, in turn, helps to curdle milk, enabling the creation of cheese, yogurt, and a number of other home dairy items.

Thermophilic Starter. This form of starter culture is considered "heat loving." Thermophilic cultures can withstand temperatures of up to 132°F (56°C), making them ideal for making hard Italian cheeses, such as Parmesan and Romano, and Swiss-type cheeses.

Acknowledgments

An overflowing garden of gratitude is in order for the many talented individuals who pulled together this project.

To the wonderful profilees: Patrick Barber, Dave Bauer, Kelly Carambula, Sarah Easterling, Tina Glenn, Denise Hale, Claudia Lucero, Jeff Norombaba, Cynthia Sharpe, and Heather Watkins-Jones. Thank you all for bringing light to the many different ways we can all enjoy the benefits of home dairy in our lives.

I applaud Rebecca Springer for waving her copyediting wand over my words with grace and good judgment.

Photographer Lynne Harty never ceased to surprise with her ability to get just the right shot over and over again. Designer Eric Stevens should be lauded for his beautiful design, illustrations, and flawless ability to pull all of the puzzle pieces together in just the right way. Abundant gratitude is offered to Chris Bryant for his invaluable design guidance and food styling prowess. Thanks to both Chris and his partner Skip Wade for generously offering up their beautiful home for the demanding but tasty photo shoot.

Heartfelt thanks to Nicole McConville, for believing I had both the skills and gumption to take on this book and the series. I am immeasurably grateful to have such a great friend and editor wrapped up in one convenient package.

For my long-suffering, infinitely patient husband, Glenn, who served as cheerleader, therapist, and official taster through all of this, I appreciate you more than you could ever know.

Finally, special thanks to Meaghan Finnerty, Paige Gilchrist, and Marcus Leaver, for all of the excitement surrounding the series that you have nurtured and enabled.

Also Available in the Homemade Living series:

Photo Credits

The pages of this book are richer thanks to the contributed photos. Much gratitude is owed to the following individuals: Aaron Carambula (page 107), Andre Garant (page 17), Josh Hale (page 102), Gerry-Anna Jones (page 29), Chris Love (page 51), Holly McGuire (page 57), Ben Melger (page 16), Amy Mostwill (page 63), Rebecca Picard (page 127), Courtney Havran Regan (page 41), Rhonda Rolle (page 39), and Sarah Shevett (page 17).

Index